T0207261

Mastering Zoho CRM

Manage your Team, Pipeline, and Clients Effectively

Ali Shabdar

Apress®

Mastering Zoho CRM: Manage your Team, Pipeline, and Clients Effectively

Ali Shabdar
Vancouver, British Columbia, Canada

ISBN-13 (pbk): 978-1-4842-2903-3   ISBN-13 (electronic): 978-1-4842-2904-0
DOI 10.1007/978-1-4842-2904-0

Library of Congress Control Number: 2017953098

Cover image designed by Freepik

Managing Director: Welmoed Spahr
Editorial Director: Todd Green
Acquisitions Editor: Louise Corrigan
Development Editor: James Markham
Technical Reviewer: Massimo Nardone
Coordinating Editor: Nancy Chen
Copy Editor: Karen Jameson
Compositor: SPi Global
Indexer: SPi Global
Artist: SPi Global

Distributed to the book trade worldwide by Springer Science+Business Media New York, 233 Spring Street, 6th Floor, New York, NY 10013. Phone 1-800-SPRINGER, fax (201) 348-4505, e-mail orders-ny@springer-sbm.com, or visit www.springeronline.com. Apress Media, LLC is a California LLC and the sole member (owner) is Springer Science + Business Media Finance Inc (SSBM Finance Inc). SSBM Finance Inc is a **Delaware** corporation.

For information on translations, please e-mail rights@apress.com, or visit http://www.apress.com/rights-permissions.

Apress titles may be purchased in bulk for academic, corporate, or promotional use. eBook versions and licenses are also available for most titles. For more information, reference our Print and eBook Bulk Sales web page at http://www.apress.com/bulk-sales.

Any source code or other supplementary material referenced by the author in this book is available to readers on GitHub via the book's product page, located at www.apress.com/9781484229033. For more detailed information, please visit http://www.apress.com/source-code.

Printed on acid-free paper

Dedication

To all unsung heroes: CRM managers, admins, consultants, business analysts, and process managers who meticulously and patiently create and maintain strong information systems for salespeople to go out there and do their magic, without worrying about what happens in the background.

Contents at a Glance

About the Author xiii

About the Technical Reviewer xv

Foreword xvii

Introduction xix

■Chapter 1: Zoho Suite from 10,000 Feet 1

■Chapter 2: CRM at Your Business Core 21

■Chapter 3: Getting Started with Zoho CRM 39

■Chapter 4: Running Your Business on Zoho CRM 61

■Chapter 5: Take Control of Marketing 131

■Chapter 6: Integrating CRM with Zoho Ecosystem 159

■Chapter 7: Taking CRM and Your Business to the Next Level 177

Index 239

Contents

About the Author xiii

About the Technical Reviewer xv

Foreword xvii

Introduction xix

■Chapter 1: Zoho Suite from 10,000 Feet 1

Sales and Marketing Apps.. 2

CRM 2

SalesInbox 3

SalesIQ.. 3

Survey... 4

Campaigns.. 4

Sites.. 5

Social.. 5

Contact Manager 6

Forms 6

Motivator 7

Email and Collaboration Apps... 7

Mail... 7

Notebook 8

Docs.. 8

Projects... 8

Connect... 9

BugTracker 9

Meeting 10

Vault 10

Showtime 11

Chat 11

Business Process Apps 11

Creator 11

AppCreator 12

Reports 13

Site24x7 13

Finance Apps 13

Books 13

Invoice 14

Subscriptions 14

Expense 15

Inventory 15

IT and Help Desk Apps 15

Desk 15

Assist 16

ServiceDesk Plus 16

Mobile Device Management 17

Human Resources Apps 17

Recruit 17

People 18

Where to Start 18

Summary 19

■Chapter 2: CRM at Your Business Core 21

The Why, the What, and the How 21

CRM 22

Beyond CRM 23

   ERP 23

   BPM 24

Process, Process, Process... 24

   Map All Processes 25

   How to Map Processes 26

Getting Started with Process Mapping... 28

   A Dash of BPMN 2.0... 28

   Your First Process Map... 30

Summary... 37

■Chapter 3: Getting Started with Zoho CRM.................................... 39

Getting Started 39

Quick Tour of the Homepage 42

CRM Terminology... 43

CRM Modules 44

Setting Up Zoho CRM 46

   User Management 51

   Email Settings.. 54

   Enabling SalesInbox 58

Summary... 60

■Chapter 4: Running Your Business on Zoho CRM 61

Managing the Sales Pipeline... 61

   Leads 62

   Lead Qualification... 62

   Opportunities 63

Getting Started with Sales Force Automation 63

Managing Leads 65

    Adding a New Lead 65

    Interacting with Leads 68

    Importing Multiple Leads 71

    Bulk Operations 77

Finding Leads 83

    Searching for Leads 83

    Filtering Through Leads 85

    Views 86

Converting Leads 92

    Deals 96

Quotes 102

    Emailing Quotes 107

    Customized Templates 109

    Converting Quotes to Sales Orders 116

    Converting Sales Orders to Invoices 117

Reports 120

    Using Existing Reports 120

    Creating New Reports 123

Forecasting Your Business 126

    Creating Your First Forecast 127

Summary 130

■Chapter 5: Take Control of Marketing 131

Marketing in the World of Micromoments 131

Campaign Management 132

    Creating Campaigns 132

    Customizing Campaigns Module 135

    Adding Leads to Campaigns 136

Webforms 138

    Creating a Webform 139

Mass Email 150

    Sending Mass Emails 151

    Sending Schedules Mass Email 154

Zoho CRM for Google AdWords 155

Zoho Suite Marketing Arsenal 155

    Email Marketing with Zoho Campaigns 155

    Managing Social Media Channels with Zoho Social 156

    Collecting Customer Feedback with Zoho Survey 156

Summary 157

■Chapter 6: Integrating CRM with Zoho Ecosystem 159

All the Zoho Integrations 159

Integrating with Zoho Mail 160

    Sharing Emails with Other CRM Users 161

Integrating with Zoho Projects 163

Integrating with Zoho Finance Suite 167

Integrating with Zoho Creator 173

Summary 176

■Chapter 7: Taking CRM and Your Business to the Next Level 177

Security Management 177

    Managing Users 178

    Managing Profiles 180

    Managing Roles 184

    Managing Data Sharing 187

    Managing Groups 194

Automating Business Processes 196

  Workflow Automation 197

  Approvals Automation.. 205

  Blueprint 213

Custom Modules... 230

  Creating Custom Modules 230

  Accessing Custom Modules.. 235

Extending CRM Beyond Zoho Platform.. 236

Summary... 237

  One More Thing 238

Index... 239

About the Author

Ali Shabdar is a Marketing and Technology Advisor helping a number of SMEs and nonprofit organizations internationally to improve efficiency and effectiveness of their tactical and stratgeic efforts.

Ali studied Electrical Engineering, IT, Sustainability, and Marketing and has more than 15 years of experience in various industries. He spent his teenage years building software, a passion that later turned into a career and helped him to keep his edge in diverse business environments.

Working with Zoho suite since early 2008, Ali has helped many SMEs to improve productivity, improve and manage processes, run effective marketing programs, increase sales, and serve clients better by utilizing Zoho offerings.

When designing cloud-based systems, Ali utilizes his applied knowledge in business process management, user experience and usability design, databases, and computer programming, which result in well-crafted solutions for real-life problems.

He loves reading about science, business, and history; watching movies, traveling, and savoring good food (anything but Hawaiian pizza). Connect with Ali on Twitter (@shabdar), LinkedIn (https://www.linkedin.com/in/shabdar/), and Instagram (ali.n.shabdar).

About the Technical Reviewer

Massimo Nardone has more than 22 years of experience in Security, Web/Mobile development, Cloud, and IT Architecture. His true IT passions are Security and Android.

He has been programming and teaching how to program with Android, Perl, PHP, Java, VB, Python, C/C++, and MySQL for more than 20 years.

Massimo holds a Master of Science degree in Computing Science from the University of Salerno, Italy. He has worked as a Project Manager, Software Engineer, Research Engineer, Chief Security Architect, Information Security Manager, PCI/SCADA Auditor, and Senior Lead IT Security/Cloud/SCADA Architect for many years.

Technical skills include Security, Android, Cloud, Java, MySQL, Drupal, Cobol, Perl, Web and Mobile development, MongoDB, D3, Joomla, Couchbase, C/C++, WebGL, Python, Pro Rails, Django CMS, Jekyll, Scratch, etc.

He currently works as Chief Information Security Officer (CISO) for Cargotec Oyj. He has worked as a visiting lecturer and supervisor for exercises at the Networking Laboratory of the Helsinki University of Technology (Aalto University). He holds four international patents (PKI, SIP, SAML, and Proxy areas).

Massimo has reviewed more than 40 IT books for different publishing companies and is the coauthor of *Pro Android Games* (Apress, 2015).

Foreword

Want a demo? You're gonna have to wait! Wow, things sure have changed. When I worked for an up-and-coming CRM start-up in 1999, our account managers would actually use the demo of the software itself as a negotiating tool. The client would request a demo of the software and our account managers would, of course, agree to that, but not before they were able to negotiate something in return such as an introduction to the senior stakeholders, including the VP Sales and/or CEO. Today, I'm the "account manager" at my company, Gloo, and I can't imagine using a demo in that way. As a matter of fact, no one asks me for a demo anymore! Why? Because they've typically already subscribed online to a full trial of the software, maybe added some data to it, and played in the system a bit. That is, they've given themselves a demo! And all this before I've even spoken to them. By the time they engage with me, they are often close to making up their mind as to which system they're going to go with and are just looking to us for guidance at this point.

I'm sure you have a similar story to the one above as to how sales in your industry have changed since the Internet has put more information in the hands of your customers. Now put cloud computing on top of this, and I'd be willing to bet that not only your sales process has changed but so has the type of person you seek to hire as a salesperson. If your people and process has changed, has your technology kept up with that change? Whether your business has a CRM system already or not, one thing is for sure: your approach to selling has been forced to adapt.

When Ali worked with Gloo a few years ago, the first thing we did was to spend time understanding clients' sales process. While our client's and our own sales process has changed, our approach to understanding that process has not. Ali's skills at not only listening to the client but even anticipating what they are trying to articulate enabled us to gain a firm understanding of the client's processes, document their processes into sometimes elaborate flowcharts, and documents that then translate these things into the foundation for their CRM system. Ali acted as a go-between the client and technical and nontechnical resources here at Gloo. You could say Ali was the glue among us all here at Gloo!

We still start all our clients with Zoho CRM as their first application. As you'll see in Ali's book, it is the hub from which other Zoho applications spoke out. Having said that, Zoho offers so much more than CRM nowadays, and our clients want access to those applications that come with pre-built integration to Zoho CRM. The market has changed as businesses demand more integration capabilities among applications and Zoho has responded with not only nearly 40 à la carte business applications (continuing to add more!), but they offer three bundles of Zoho CRM Plus, Zoho Workplace, and Zoho Finance Plus – and didn't stop there! You can now purchase all Zoho applications in the Zoho One bundle.

One thing that hasn't changed since CRM emerged in the late 1990s is that despite its user-friendly interface, it's a complex machine and you're going to need help setting it up properly for your business. Reading all the "online help" files in the world would still require you to decide where to start and where to go next. Engaging with a consultancy like Gloo allows our team to guide you through it all. However, if you like the DIY approach, Ali has done the heavy lifting for you by writing a step-by-step guide that will help you begin to walk through the maze of CRM. This book sets a great foundation for you to build on, and I highly recommend it no matter how you approach your project!

Wishing you all the best in your business and your CRM project,

Lorin Bourassa
Gloo
www.gloocrm.com

Introduction

Before I started working on this book, I had a look at the first book I wrote on *Zoho, Foundation Zoho: Work and Create Online* (Apress, 2009), and I was amazed by how far we have come since then.

Technology has advanced so much in less than a decade that 2009 feels like ages ago. Smartphones, big data, Blockchain, 3D printing, civilian drones, artificial intelligence, and Internet of Things (IoT), have all graduated lab life and entered our daily lives.

However, none of these technologies (yet) have had as great of an impact on our civilization as cloud computing. This may sound like a very bold claim, but bear with me for a moment.

Many of us nowadays keep our collection of documents on Dropbox or Google Drive, kill time (or do something more productive) on Instagram and Facebook, and rely on CRMs (Customer Relationship Management systems) to manage our sales processes, take notes on Wunderlist, and manage projects on Trello.

Back in 2009, cloud computing was a relatively new phenomenon, and many companies, small, or large, were too hesitant to even give it a try. High speed Internet was not as ubiquitous as it is now and mobile computing was at its infancy. Heck, Blackberry was the king of the smartphones.

All these are courtesy of some SaaS (software as a service) on a public cloud platform. Remove cloud computing from the equation, and you won't be able to even play Pokémon Go on your smartphone.

Eight years later, Internet connectivity has doubled,[1] and almost half of the population of the planet are connected. Today, it is practically impossible to go through a full day (sometimes a full hour) without using the amazing apps and services that run on the cloud. But what is cloud computing anyway?

Cloud Computing

The Internet, as it is referred to as the Cloud in IT jargon, powers today's civilization.

Why on earth the IT crowd would use the word "cloud" as a metaphor for the Internet, you ask? Since the old days, it was common when someone wanted to refer to a big collection of servers (i.e., server farm) in an IT diagram, they would simply draw a cloud to hide the complexity and just connect other machines to it (see Figure 1 for a rough idea).

---

[1]http://www.internetlivestats.com/internet-users/

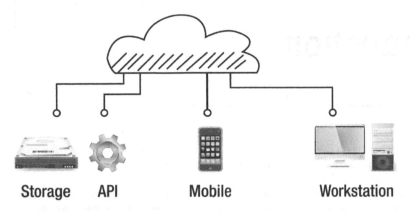

Figure 1. *The Cloud*

Cloud computing, to put it simply, is to use the computing power of the cloud in combination, or instead of, with the power of the computer on your desk or the one in your pocket. As trivial as this definition may sound, cloud computing offers unique features, such as the following:

- Availability - All you need is an Internet connection to connect to any cloud anywhere.

- Performance - The immense power of thousands of servers is at your disposal.

- Elasticity - You could only use and pay for the computing power and storage you need for the task in hand, scale up when you need more resources, and scale back down when you don't.

- Multi-Tenancy - Multiple tenants (apps, services, users, etc.) can use the power of a cloud, allowing resources to be used efficiently and costs to be divided between such tenants.

- Security - Clouds can be way more secure than your local computer, or local server. Since cloud providers have many more resources to allocate safeguarding their infrastructure, which in turn keeps the tenants more secure.

- Reliability - Your data is backed up and is available across multiple physical locations, minimizing the risk of data loss to almost zero.

- Maintenance - Cloud users (tenants) need not worry about upgrading servers, power outages, or software updates, all of which are done for you by the cloud provider.

- Cost - Of course, all of the above contribute to a major benefit of cloud computing, which is lowering the cost across the board.

In general, there are three types of clouds:

- public, which as the name suggests, are publicly available for everyone to utilize, such as Amazon AWS;

- private cloud, which is only accessible to an organization or organizations owning that cloud; and

- hybrid cloud, which obviously, is a combination of public and private clouds.

■ **Note** I stay shallow with these definitions as this book is not about the science of cloud computing. The main audience for this book is businesspeople that I can bet are least interested in the voodoo behind the technology and merely want to utilize tools that can make their lives easier.

The Importance and Scale of Cloud Computing

As mentioned before, it is safe to say that anything digital nowadays runs on some sort of cloud infrastructure. Our civilization depends on the cloud, an industry that is poised to grow to $270 billion by the year 2020.[2]

In their 2009 report, "Cloud Computing Forecasting Change",[3] Deloitte called cloud computing the "next technological disruption to transform enterprise IT delivery and services." It is a brilliant piece, which counts cloud computing along with social networks, mobile, and Internet of Things (IoT) among the major disruptors and contributors to the maturity of the Internet.

Deloitte's prediction about cloud computing was impressively accurate, except that Deloitte and many other experts did not quite predict, however, what was the great impact and massive adoption of cloud computing on small- to medium-size businesses (SMBs).

In January 2016, RightScale surveyed 1,060 technical professionals (627 from SMBs) about how their adoption of cloud computing.[4] The results are, astonishingly, a testament to how successful cloud computing has been in recent years:

- 77% of the SMBs are using cloud computing in some capacity in their organizations;

- Only 9% said they have no plans for cloud adoption;

- Cloud security is no longer the top challenge, dethroned now by lack of resources and expertise;

---

[2]http://247wallst.com/technology-3/2015/03/07/
the-270-billon-cloud-computing-market/
[3]http://public.deloitte.no/dokumenter/2_Cloud_Computing%5B1%5D.pdf
[4]http://assets.rightscale.com/uploads/pdfs/RightScale-2016-State-of-the-Cloud-
Report.pdf

- Cloud users leverage six clouds on average; and

- Amazon AWS leads the pack while Microsoft Azure is growing is market share as major cloud infrastructure providers.

At its core, cloud computing allows organizations (and individuals) to harness the virtually unlimited computing and storage power of hundreds of thousands of servers located in a myriad of data centers across the world.

It is, with the immense power of cloud at our fingertips, possible that even the smallest companies can analyze terabytes of data at will, fast, and cheap, to create massively useful applications and stay ahead of the competition.

Companies such as Uber, Airbnb, Waze, Instagram, Snapchat, and hundreds of others whose apps you use on a daily basis all started small, writing their apps on top of cloud platforms. The start-up revolution in the past decade owes its success heavily to the availability, affordability, and scalability of cloud platforms such as Amazon AWS, Google AppEngine, and Microsoft Azure.

Now with the next wave of computing, mainstream AI (Artificial Intelligence), upon us, companies such as Amazon are working to make it possible for the software developers and cloud users to have access to sophisticated AI capabilities on the cheap.[5]

The Service Economy

Cloud computing allows various services and applications to be implemented on it. This allows a "service" model in which virtually everything can be offered as a service that is implemented and distributed on some sort of a cloud. This concept is called Everything as a Service or X as a Service (XaaS).

Platform as a Service (PaaS) and Infrastructure as a Service (IaaS) are two examples of what can be offered as a service in the cloud. But the most evident and most relevant to of all these to the end user (including you, dear reader) is Software as a Service (SaaS).

Let's start with a real-life example.

A few years ago, if I needed Microsoft Office I had to pay full price for it just to buy and own the software before I could use it. A few hundred dollars wouldn't break the bank, but now imagine if I wanted to have Office on all of my 15 workstations at work. Then I would have had to commit to a few thousand dollars only in basic software expenses. Plus, I would need to have IT take care of updates and patches (more expense) and then pay again for every major version released.

Today, with Office 365, not only do I always have access to the latest version of the Office software on my laptop, tablet, and phone with the same license, but also software updates run more automatically, I get to use 1TB (yes, that is 1000 Gigabytes) of free space on OneCloud (Microsoft's cloud storage service), plus I have access to all my documents with editing capability in the browser.

That means I can leave my laptop at home and go on a vacation and edit my documents wherever there is a computer connected to the Internet. The best part? I pay a fraction of the cost on a monthly basis and I can cancel my contract anytime I want.

---

[5]http://www.allthingsdistributed.com/2016/11/amazon-ai-and-alexa-for-all-aws-apps.html

The same applies for my company. I pay for a new monthly license when someone joins the team, and I cancel their contract when someone leaves.

This is the power of Software as a Service, or SaaS.

Unlike Microsoft Office, the majority of SaaS apps do not even need to be installed on your local computer. You can access them on a modern Internet browser on a desktop, laptop, tablet, or a mobile device.

The main advantage here is that SaaS doesn't rely much on local computer power, so you don't need a high-performance machine to run your massive CRM used by 2000 employees across 3 continents. A $200 Chromebook[6] will do the job too.

This book is about one of these SaaS applications, Zoho CRM. By the end of this book, you will have learned how you can transform your core business processes and stay productive using one of the best SaaS applications out there.

Zoho

Zoho, the company behind Zoho CRM and an impressive suite of 34 other SaaS apps has been in business since 1996. Launched back in November 2005, Zoho CRM is one of Zoho's main offerings and arguably one of the most powerful and widely used ones.

▪ **Note**   You can read more about the history of Zoho and the brains behind it on their website: https://www.zoho.com/aboutus.html.

I have been an avid user of Zoho suite, especially Zoho CRM and Zoho Creator since 2008. I have recommended Zoho to many friends, colleagues, and clients, all of whom have ended up becoming happy users. Powerful and easy-to-use apps, cost effectiveness, and good support have been some of the main factors that have kept thousands of organizations and individuals as loyal customers.

I hope this book helps you in deciding whether Zoho CRM is the right choice for you, and if it is, how to best utilize it in your day-to-day business.

Who Is This Book for?

This book is for everyone who cares about the growth of their business, or is fully, or partly, in charge of generating sales for their company. If you are the slightest serious about the current and future state of your business, CRM must be at the core of your business regardless of the size or the business model.

This book is for you if any of the following applies to you:

- still rely on your inbox, contact list app, or spreadsheets to manage your clients;

- are confused whether you need a CRM, or believe CRM is overkill for your operation;

---

[6]https://www.google.com/chromebook/about/

- are deciding which CRM is the suitable choice for your business;

- don't have the budget to spend thousands of dollars on expensive celebrity CRMs out there;

- want to set up your own CRM, learn how to manage it, and do great things with it;

- want to make a living providing CRM consultancy; or

- are already a Zoho CRM user, administrator, or solution provider wanting to learn more about it.

Running a successful business is about delighting your customers and you can't delight your customers unless you provide a seamless experience for them before, during, and after they have bought your products or services. CRM, and Zoho CRM in particular, will help you achieve that goal.

What You Are Going to Learn

In this book, you will learn the following:

- Set up Zoho CRM properly from the ground up;

- Model your business processes and implement them on Zoho CRM;

- Centralize and manage your entire marketing, sales, and customer service processes;

- Integrate CRM with other Zoho tools to streamline day-to-day business operations;

- Create powerful dashboards and reports to provide relevant and actionable information;

- Use advanced CRM features such as workflow automation, role-based security, and data sharing;

- Connect Zoho CRM to external tools and services to extend features; and

- Let CRM scale up with your business needs and help you grow.

How the Book Is Structured

The aim of this book is to provide you with a quick but effective guide to make Zoho CRM work for business, regardless of your business size. Chapters are focused on step-by-step guides to get you up and running in the subject matter discussed while giving you tips, always having the bigger picture in mind.

Throughout the book there are frequent references to the official documentation as it wouldn't make sense to cover every single feature or capability of Zoho CRM in a single volume. Also, Zoho CRM, like any other cloud-based app, adds new features. It is a good habit to check the documentation often and stay up to speed with the developments.

Chapters of the Book

This book starts with a quick review of the Zoho suite of cloud-based apps in Chapter 1. This chapter will give you a brief idea of what other Zoho apps you could be using in your business.

In Chapter 2 we will take a step back and briefly look at the philosophy of CRM and how being on top your business processes is the key to success in implementing a successful CRM and also winning in business in the long run.

In Chapter 3, you will be setting up Zoho CRM from the ground up and cover essentials, such as user and email management.

Chapter 4 will take you through a complete journey of managing your sales pipeline, starting from mere leads, opportunities, and deals to conversions, reports, and forecasts. This chapter will show you the power and ease of use of Zoho CRM available to you, out of the box.

In Chapter 5, an important and often ignored aspect of a successful CRM system will be discussed: marketing. You will learn how Zoho CRM and other Zoho tools can offer a complete platform for your marketing efforts.

Chapter 6 is focused on extending the power of Zoho CRM by integrating it with other Zoho tools you learned about in Chapter 1.

More advanced topics will be covered in Chapter 7, focused more on features available exclusively to the top tiers of Zoho CRM. Role-based security, data sharing, and business process automation are among the topics discussed in the chapter.

How to Best Read This Book

If you are new to Zoho CRM, or the subject of CRM in general, I highly recommend you start from the beginning and follow the order of the chapters.

Unless you are experienced in business process and have done a few process maps in the past, make sure you go through Chapter 2. It is worth stopping at the end of Chapter 2 and learning more about business process improvement and business process management as it will help you set up a successful CRM for your organization. Even if you already have Zoho CRM installed for your business, it is worth going back and reviewing all processes for efficiency and effectiveness.

Chapters 3, 6, and 7 will particularly help you as a CRM manager, admin, or consultant to get the most out of Zoho CRM.

If you are sharing this book with your staff that will be using (not configuring or managing) CRM, ask them to focus on Chapter 4 and learn pipeline management, the Zoho CRM way.

CHAPTER 1

■ ■ ■

Zoho Suite from 10,000 Feet

Zoho Corporation has come a long way since they released their first SaaS apps, Writer and CRM, in 2005. Writer became the inseparable part of the productivity apps and CRM has grown to be of the core Zoho products today, serving millions of people around the world, yours truly included.

From the app diversity and completeness of offerings perspective, Zoho still holds a unique and strong position in the market while other companies have focused on one or a few products around a core objective.

There are many fantastic SaaS apps out there; however, none of which I used or read about offer the selection Zoho does. This allows users to use a wide range of apps with a single sign on, familiar look and feel, and interoperability (i.e., ability to exchange and use information between apps) out of the box.

Zoho apps are divided into six categories:

- Sales and Marketing

- Email and Collaboration

- Business Process

- Finance

- IT and Help Desk

- Human Resources

Now lets' have a very quick look at each one of these categories and their respective apps.

■ **Note** This chapter merely scratches the surface and only provides a quick introduction of all members of the Zoho suite. The aim is to simply let you know what each app can do and leave further investigation to you to see whether one or more of these apps could help your business in any way.

© Ali Shabdar 2017
A. Shabdar, *Mastering Zoho CRM*, DOI 10.1007/978-1-4842-2904-0_1

Sales and Marketing Apps

The beating heart of any business, be it a home-based solo operation or a multinational conglomerate, is sales. Marketing, on the other hand, provides insights of the market and helps the business stay competitive while promoting its products and services to the world. The duo of Marketing and Sales is inseparable.

At the core of the Zoho suite, there are a number of apps that help you manage almost all your marketing and sales operations, all connected in the cloud.

CRM

Zoho CRM is arguably the star of the show with the highest number of users among Zoho apps. First released in 2005, CRM has grown from a small solution for beginners to a full-fledged suite of an application competing with the industry leaders on many fronts.

The landscape of cloud-based CRM systems for small- and medium-size businesses is quite competitive, and there are formidable contenders in the market for every requirement and budget. The spectrum of SaaS CRM systems seems endless with open source and free offerings inside of the spectrum to full-fledged industry-specific solutions on the other hand. Bitrix24, Highrise, Hubspot, Infusionsoft, Insightly, Microsoft Dynamics, Pipedrive, Salesforce, and Sugar CRM are just a few that come to mind.

Well, this book is about Zoho CRM, so I know which one I will be recommending. That said, Zoho CRM may not be an answer for everyone. The premise of this book is that CRM is one of the most important, if not the most important tool, for your business. So, choosing the right one early on is crucial.

We will see how Zoho CRM addresses the requirements of a wide range of businesses. No matter if you are about to start your business in a month, currently bootstrapping, or you have been in business for the past 15 years managing a team of 100 salespeople across the globe, Zoho CRM can play a key role in managing and streamlining your marketing, sales, and client servicing efforts.

Zoho CRM offers five different editions with each packing a host of features suitable for different tastes and needs:

- **Free edition:** This edition offers the core modules such as Leads, Accounts, Contacts, Feeds, Documents, and mobile apps for up to 10 users, completely free of charge. This is a great way to start using Zoho CRM and upgrade to one of the paid editions as your business needs grow.

- **Standard edition:** In addition to the features available in the Free edition, you will have access to sales forecasting, reports and dashboards, document library, roles and profiles, mass email, call center connectors, and the ability to store up to 100,000 records of information.

- **Professional edition:** Similarly, the Professional edition offers all the features available in Free and Standard editions, plus email integration, social features, Google AdWords integration, workflow automation, inventory management, macros, and the ability to store unlimited records.

- **Enterprise edition:** This edition offers territory management, custom applications, custom buttons, workflow approval processes, page layouts, custom modules, and multiple currencies on top of the features available to the Professional edition.

- **Ultimate edition:** Last, but not least, the Ultimate edition adds even more features to make it the choice for larger organizations by throwing in sandbox, dedicated database cluster, priority support, advanced customization, advanced CRM analytics, and enhanced storage.

- **CRM Plus:** A recent addition to the CRM family, CRM Plus provides a more holistic approach to the traditional CRM system by combining the Enterprise edition with Zoho Campaigns, Desk, SalesIQ, Social, Projects, Survey, and Reports. This package allows users to centralize all their marketing, sales, and client servicing processes in one place without the need to jump between different platforms while saving considerably in direct and indirect costs.

■ **Note**   Don't worry if the modules and features mentioned above don't make sense to you yet. We will be exploring almost all of these and use them in the examples of this book.

One of the areas Zoho CRM excels in, compared to the rivals, is a lower barrier to entry. Zoho CRM allows organizations of up to 10 employees to use it free of charge for sales management and later upgrade to a suitable paid edition as they need more features.

SalesInbox

A new addition to the Zoho suite, SalesInbox claims to be the first mailbox specifically designed for salespeople. According to Zoho, SalesInbox automatically organizes and prioritizes sales activities based on the sales pipeline and the stage in which each deal is. Using Zoho CRM criteria and rules features, SalesInbox could become a sales team's best friend and put an end to the manual work between email and CRM.

■ **Reference**   To learn more about SalesInbox, check out https://www.zoho.com/salesinbox/?src=zoho-snm.

SalesIQ

Zoho SalesIQ is a live chat solution that you can install and enable on your website to understand how visitors are interacting with your website in real time. It provides the visitors of your website with a familiar chat box placed on a corner of a webpage, so they can ask the sales or support team for help right away, or leave a message without leaving the page.

You can use SalesIQ in conjunction with Zoho CRM and streamline the conversion of site visitors to prospects and ultimately buying customers. You should consider using SalesIQ if you are serious about capturing website visitors and turning them into customers or providing them with an interactive support channel.

The Free edition provides a decent set of features for you to get up and running with SalesIQ and later upgrade to one of the paid editions as your requirements grow.

■ **Reference**   To learn more about SalesIQ, check out `https://www.zoho.com/salesiq/help/`.

Survey

Zoho Survey is a versatile tool to create online surveys and collect information from leads, prospects, or existing clients through a number of questions. You can dispatch surveys on your website, via mobile, or email and have the collected information from these channels store in the back end of Survey for later analysis.

Apart from standard survey building and distributing features, Zoho Survey automatically translates your surveys to 30 languages,[1] and integrates well with email campaign apps such as Zoho Campaigns and MailChimp.

■ **Reference**   To learn more about Zoho Survey, check out `https://www.zoho.com/survey/help/`.

Campaigns

Another powerful app in Zoho's arsenal is Campaigns, which offers all the tools you need to run successful email campaigns. It integrates well with other core Zoho apps, especially CRM, removing the need for third-party solutions in most cases.

Any modern organization needs to include email marketing in some shape or form in their business practice. Staying in touch with customers as well as prospects is crucial and Campaigns allows you to do just that. Despite social media being a major channel for connecting with your audience, email still remains the most effective way of communication and making sales happen.

Moreover, Campaigns offers email templates to get you up and running in minutes, plus email automation features to save you time and help your campaigns be more effective. It also provides you with detailed campaign reporting tools for monitoring and fine-tuning your efforts.

There is a free edition that allows storing up to 2,000 contacts and sending up to 12,000 emails every month, so you have little excuse not to start sending that monthly newsletter that you have been delaying.

---

[1]`https://www.zoho.com/survey/translate-survey.html`

> ■ **Reference**   To learn more about Zoho Campaigns, check out `https://www.zoho.com/campaigns/help/`.

Sites

Unless you are visiting us from a planet where websites are so passé, you most probably have a website for your business and chances are that setting it up was not particularly a pleasant experience.

There was a time, not so long ago, that if you needed a visually bearable and decently functional website, you either needed to know some graphic design and also coding in HTML, CSS, and JavaScript (three of the main technologies behind every website), or you were at the mercy of web design companies and freelancers.

Times have changed for the better. Now everyone can build a usable website that looks modern, has most of the functionalities of a business website, and works on mobile phones as well. Services such as Weebly and Wix allow you to simply drag and drop building blocks on webpage skeletons and create a website ready for prime time. Zoho, too, happens to have their own website creation wizard: Zoho Sites.

Zoho Sites provides you with a platform to easily and quickly create a professional looking website with all the modern features you need, such as blogs, social, multimedia, e-commerce, and forms.

What is great is that you can do all of these without writing a single line of code or knowing what the difference between HTTP and HTML is.

Similar to other Zoho apps, you can start with a free plan, which offers enough features to get your website up and running; and opt for the paid, more feature-rich edition down the road.

> ■ **Reference**   To learn more about Zoho Sites, check out `https://zohosites.wiki.zoho.com/`.

Social

Social media management has become a part of the business routine of every forward-thinking business. The immense power of social media allows you to delight prospects and clients by conveying a more personal and conversational message across multiple channels.

With a multitude of available social channels, however, it is hard to stay on top of publishing, monitoring, and responding to communications and staying productive and keeping your sanity in the process.

Fortunately, there are tools that help you manage social media, including Zoho Social, a capable social management tool. As of this writing, it allows you to centrally manage Twitter, Facebook, LinkedIn, Google+, and Instagram.

You, and your team collaboratively, can publish on selected channels in one go, schedule messages, and monitor the performance of your messages. You can also listen to a social channel for what people are saying about your business or personal brand.

Another useful feature of Social is that it connects to Zoho CRM effortlessly and improves your productivity by providing you with contextual information about your social connections that may be on the CRM as well.

As usual, you can start with Zoho Social free of charge and upgrade to a paid plan when you need more features.

■ **Reference**　To learn more about Zoho Social, check out `https://www.zoho.com/social/help/`.

Contact Manager

Having a stand-alone app for managing your contacts may seem totally unnecessary, but don't mistake Zoho Contact Manager for your average contact on your laptop or smartphone.

Contact Manager is actually a mini CRM allowing you to store and manage your contact database more effectively. You can share contacts within your team, define and assign tasks and follow-ups around contacts, manage deals related to contacts, and integrate your contact database with third-party services such as Google Apps or MailChimp.

If you believe you don't need a full-fledged CRM solution, Contact Manager is a great way to start introducing order to your sales processes and centralizing valuable client information.

■ **Reference**　To learn more about Zoho Contact Manger, check out `https://www.zoho.com/contactmanager/help.html`.

Forms

Sometimes you need to collect information (online) from staff members, local community, clients, or your website visitors. To do so, you usually place some sort of a form on a webpage and encourage people to fill it up and submit it back to you.

However, not all forms are created equally. A form could be a simple *Contact Us* form, a long survey, or a complex form with automation workflows embedded for approval collection.

Traditionally, you or someone you hire would need web programming knowledge to create a form with such capabilities. With Zoho Forms, all you need to do is to drag and drop the form fields to a form, do some configurations, and then publish your modern-looking form online for people to populate.

Zoho Forms allows you to quickly create functional forms, collect data, analyze the performance of your forms, and integrate them with Zoho apps, such as CRM; or third-party apps, such as MailChimp, to automate tedious data entry tasks.

Again, you can start using Zoho Forms for free and upgrade to a paid edition as your requirements grow.

■ **Reference**   To learn more about Forms, check out https://www.zoho.com/forms/ help/getting-started.html.

Motivator

Another newcomer to the Zoho suite, Motivator, is a sales activity management tool. It allows you to set sales targets and KPIs (Key Performance Indicators) for your team, then it automatically analyzes sale information extracted from Zoho CRM to generate team member performance so that top salespeople are identified, acknowledged, and rewarded for their achievements.

Motivator has a feature called TV Channels, which allows you to show a leaderboard of your team performance on big screen TVs to motivate the team and encourage employees to compete in a healthy and rewarding environment.

■ **Reference**   To learn more about Zoho Motivator, check out https://www.zoho.com/ motivator/help/.

Email and Collaboration Apps

To complement the core apps mentioned above, Zoho offers essential apps helping you manage your emails, projects, and documents, all improved for the Internet age and built from ground up to house modern features, such as social and collaboration features.

A number of other apps help you stay connected with your team and perform a number of essential tasks, such as safely storing your passwords in a centralized location.

Mail

Zoho Mail is Zoho's answer to popular services such as Gmail, or Outlook.com. Although it may be much less popular compered other old timers, it is arguably one of the easiest to use and most feature-rich mail services in the market. Plus, it is ad-free. No more pesky ads in the sanctity of your inbox, ever.

In addition to the default web interface, Mail offers native smartphone apps for iOS and Android. You can also configure your favorite desktop or mobile email client (Spark, Outlook, Apple Mail, etc.) to check your Zoho account emails.

For business users, Zoho Mail integrates well with other Zoho services such as CRM. You can enjoy a single sign-on feature (one user account to use multiple services) and host one domain (i.e., yourwebsite.com), plus up to 25 users, all free of charge.

■ **Reference**   To learn more about Zoho Mail, check out `https://www.zoho.com/mail/help/`.

Notebook

Notetaking apps are everywhere. Many of them are average at best, and some of them are amazing. Good notetaking apps, such as Evernote and Microsoft OneNote can massively contribute to your productivity and help you minimize clutter.

Zoho offers its own version of a notetaking app, Zoho Notebook. It helps you organize your notes in a variety of formats: text, image, audio, checklists, and sketches. Notes offers a smartphone app for iOS and Android and a web clipper to capture content snippets while web surfing.

As of this writing, Zoho is yet to release a desktop version for Notebook, similar to what Evernote and Microsoft OneNote offer. As an avid Evernote user since 2009, I can see that Zoho Notebook shows promise, especially that it sports a pleasant and easy-to-use interface and is 100% free.

■ **Reference**   To learn more about Zoho Notebook, check out `https://www.zoho.com/notebook/`.

Docs

Zoho Docs is a cloud-based storage space on steroids. You can store up to 5GB of files on a free edition of Docs, sync your files between devices, and use Zoho productivity suite (Writer, Sheet, and Show) to edit your documents in the browser or via their native mobile apps.

You can download the Zoho Docs desktop synchronization tool and your documents between a local folder and the Docs folder seamlessly.

If you are already a Google Drive or Dropbox user, you will feel right at home with Zoho Docs. The free edition of Docs offers features almost identical to the free edition of Google Drive; however, the paid edition gives more bang for your buck compared to the paid edition of the Google Drive.

■ **Reference**   To learn more about Zoho Docs, check out `https://www.zoho.com/docs/resources.html`.

Projects

With hundreds of free and paid options available in the market, finding the right project management tool that covers all the bases and doesn't break the bank seems like a daunting job.

Luckily, Zoho has a powerful project management tool called Zoho Project. It offers a decent combination of ease of use, features, and cost-effectiveness making it a formidable choice in the crowded market of cloud-based project management tools.

With Zoho Projects you can run multiple projects across multiple teams, share information with clients and outsourced teams easily, create time sheets for your projects, create Gantt charts and other complex reports, collaborate seamlessly with all the stakeholders, and mange project documents and in a central environment.

You have access to your projects via browser and native mobile apps. You can also connect Projects to other apps such as Zoho Books and Zoho Invoice as well as third-party services such as Google Apps and Dropbox to maximize your productivity and efficiency.

Zoho Projects comes free of charge if you are planning to manage one project at a time. You can always upgrade to paid editions if you need more from your project management tool.

■ **Reference**   To learn more about Zoho Projects, check out `https://www.zoho.com/projects/help/`.

Connect

Zoho Connect allows you to create a private social network for your organizations. It provides you with all the basic tools and features to set up a social network for your team to connect and collaborate in real time.

By allowing you to create custom apps and integrate other services such as Zoho Projects, Zoho Docs, Google Drive, and Calendar services, Connect helps you streamline internal communications processes and keep employees engaged while boosting their productivity.

Similar to other Zoho apps, Connect offers a free edition for you to start building your organizational social network and later upgrade to paid plans if you need more features.

■ **Reference**   To learn more about Zoho Connect, check out `https://www.zoho.com/connect/resources.html`.

BugTracker

If you are into software engineering, you know that during the software life cycle, proper bug tracking is very important, and using a powerful bug tracking service will make the lives of everyone involved in the project easier.

Zoho BugTracker offers all the essential features a robust bug tracking service should provide, plus bug automation features with workflows, out-of-the-box integration with Github and BitBucket, file sharing, collaborative dashboard environment, and SLA (Service Level Automation) automation.

■ **Reference**   To learn more about Zoho BugTracker, check out https://www.zoho.com/bugtracker/help/.

Meeting

Zoho Meeting is an easy-to-use and powerful web conferencing and live collaboration tool for you to take your remote meetings to the next level. You can schedule and run unlimited meetings with up to 20 hosts (paid edition) and 100 guests (paid edition) to join your web meetings.

Zoho Meeting allows you to remotely control a participant's computer, making it a great tool for remote demoing or troubleshooting. Although there is a handy desktop plug-in, Meeting doesn't need you to install an app to run or join meetings and is completely browser based.

It also integrates well with other services such as Zoho CRM, Zoho Chat, Zoho Calendar, Google Calendar, and Google Apps.

As with most Zoho apps, you can start for free and set up one-on-one meetings right away.

■ **Reference**   To learn more about Zoho Meeting, check out https://www.zoho.com/meeting/resources.html.

Vault

We all use a myriad of apps and services every day, each requiring an account, which as prehistoric as it may be, requires a username and a password to log in. Until technology comes up with a better way of authenticating users, there is no escape from memorizing or storing account information somewhere in a secure place.

Fortunately, there are several apps and services such as 1Password, or Keychain Access in Mac OS that store our passwords for us, so we can spend our precious brain power on Candy Crush, or something less disappointing.

For teams and businesses, Zoho Vault promises to alleviate this very challenge and make password management easy. Vault manages all your passwords securely and centrally, logs you into sites and services without the need for manual password entry, allows you to share managed passwords with select team members, monitors usage of each password, and grants or denies password access accordingly.

■ **Reference**   To learn more about Zoho Vault, check out https://www.zoho.com/vault/getting-started.html.

Showtime

If you teach or train people for a living, or just give occasional presentations to a large audience, you know how important it is to keep the audience engaged and turn them into active participants during a session.

Zoho Showtime builds on this simple but crucial fact and provides a tool for you to run a smooth show while keeping your audience fully engaged during and after a session. You can motivate the audience to express their opinion, run polls, ask questions, and later when the session is over, send feedback from and monitor how people engaged with your content.

Showtime is a promising and possibly game-changing service for forward-thinking trainers. The great news is that it is available for everybody to use free of charge.

■ **Reference**   To learn more about Zoho Showtime, check out https://www.zoho.com/showtime/help/.

Chat

Zoho Chat provides a powerful communication platform for your team, free of charge, where you can create channels, share documents, and do more in a modern environment available on your computer and your mobile phone.

Zoho Chat is very easy to use and you get it up and running for your organization in a few minutes. You will feel quite at home if you used other tools such as Yammer or Slack.

■ **Reference**   To learn more about Zoho Chat, check out https://www.zoho.com/chat/help/.

Business Process Apps

Another powerful set of apps that distinguishes Zoho suite from the competition are the business process apps. Using these apps, you can build complex database applications to run your entire business, or complement other Zoho apps, such as CRM. You can also generate sophisticated business and scientific reports based on stand-alone databases or tie them back to other Zoho apps.

Creator

Zoho Creator is a powerful platform for creating fully customized cloud-based applications. If you have a specific set of business requirements that you can't find in any existing tool, or the available solutions are too expensive, too trivial, or too advanced, you can quickly create your very own solution with Creator.

One of the things that makes Creator great is that in many cases you don't need to do a single line of coding to make functional apps. Creator offers many tools to program and automate your business processes, but for simpler apps, you don't need to know any coding.

Simply drag and drop data fields (text boxes, lists, buttons, etc.) to create forms and Zoho Creator will do a lot of magic in the background to turn those forms into a full-fledged application.

My first encounter with Zoho was through Creator. Back in 2008 I was in charge of the marketing department of an international real estate brand. We had a clunky CRM system, which no one used properly, and it quickly became a bottleneck in our daily business processes. We were losing valuable information because salespeople refused to use that behemoth of a CRM.

To mitigate this, I ended up creating a mini CRM for the sales team from scratch only using Zoho Creator. The app was multiuser, secure, always available, and accessible from everywhere. It even generated listing data automatically to send to the local media for advertisement.

The team loved the app and used it even after I left that company. I could have created a web app from scratch using HTML, PHP, and MySQL, but it would have taken me a month to create, test, and deploy something usable. With Creator, I took the app from concept to launch in four days while running the marketing department.

■ **Note**   If you want to learn more about Zoho Creator and how to leverage its power to create world-class cloud-based business applications for your organization, or your client, feel free to pick up my other book, *Mastering Zoho Creator* (Apress, 2017). You will learn all the basics of app building in Creator, plus advanced material such as scripting in Deluge and integrating with other Zoho apps and third-party services.

AppCreator

Another recent addition to the Zoho family, AppCreator allows you to quickly and with minimal or no coding create native mobile apps for iOS, Android, and Windows phones and tablets.

With AppCreator you can publish your apps internally within your organization, or publicly through one of the app stores.

As of this writing, AppCreator is quite new and available via invitation only.

■ **Reference**   To learn more about Zoho Creator, check out https://www.zoho.com/appcreator/help/overview.html.

Reports

If you are into data crunching and analysis, and spreadsheets don't meet your requirements anymore, Zoho Reports is a great option to consider. We live in the age of big data and data science is the talk of the town. A plethora of powerful tools such as R, Python, and Tableau are available; however, not everyone needs the data scientist's toolbox.

Zoho Reports is one of the less-known gems that provides you with a powerful toolset for collecting data from multiple sources, performing calculations and analyses, collaborating, data visualization, and more.

Using Zoho Reports you can manage millions of records and create business intelligence to contribute to the success of your business. You can also integrate it with Zoho Creator and other apps and services.

Zoho Reports offers a free edition for you to crunch up to 100,000 records of data, plus a number of paid editions for heavier use. If you still rely on spreadsheets for data analysis and visualization, I strongly suggest you give Reports a try.

■ **Reference** To learn more about Zoho Reports, check out https://www.zoho.com/ reports/help/index.html.

Site24x7

Site24x7 is for organizations, IT professionals, and developers who want to monitor the performance and availability of websites, servers, and web applications. With a host of features to let you monitor that your business platforms are doing alright and make sure everything stays in check, Site24x7 could be a great help to your business.

■ **Reference** To learn more about Zoho Site24x7, check out https://www.site24x7. com/contact-support.html.

Finance Apps

No business can afford ignoring to manage finances properly. As you might have guessed, Zoho has you covered. A number of finance-related apps will help you keep track of your expenses, manage complex accounting operations, issue invoices, and streamline how you get paid by clients. There is even an app for managing your inventory, albeit, it may not quite fit under the "finance" category.

Books

Zoho Books is a powerful, yet affordable, accounting software in the cloud. With Books, you get all the features you (or your accountants) expect from an accounting and bookkeeping software, plus a host of other useful features.

You can issue customized invoices and accept online payments via a service such as PayPal, connect to your bank accounts for automated cash flow and account monitoring, create powerful reports that management and clients can understand, track your inventory, and let clients see what concerns them during a project.

You can also connect Zoho Books to other apps such as Zoho CRM, Projects, and Reports and make them all operate as a big connected system to manage your entire business.

To make your life easier, Books offers mobile and smartwatch apps, so you are always up to speed with what is happening in your business financially.

■ **Reference**   To learn more about Zoho Books, check out `https://www.zoho.com/books/support/`.

Invoice

If you are happy with your current accounting software or don't really need a complete accounting software, Zoho Books may not seem so appealing. Sometimes all you need as a solopreneur or freelancer is to be able to issue an invoice now and then. In this case, Zoho Invoice may just be the answer.

With Invoice, you can define your products and services, add clients, and quickly issue estimates and invoices. You can also customize your invoices to your liking and include the option to get paid online from within the invoice you send to clients.

Moreover, you can track expenses, set up reminders for your customers to pay you on time, and track time for your projects, so you can get paid accurately for the amount of work you put in.

The good news is that you can start using Zoho Invoice for free for up to 25 clients with all the features available to you.

■ **Reference**   To learn more about Zoho Invoice, check out `https://www.zoho.com/invoice/support/`.

Subscriptions

If you have recurring billing in your business, for example, you accept monthly payments for the subscription site you run, then Zoho Subscriptions can take care of the entire back end of the payment system for you.

With Subscriptions, you can create your pricing model, automate billing and payment management, monitor your payments, and make strategic decisions accordingly.

Zoho Subscriptions connects to most of the common payment gateways such as PayPal and Stripe, and, of course, Zoho apps such as CRM and Books to make your life easier.

■ **Reference**   To learn more about Zoho Subscriptions, check out `https://www.zoho.com/subscriptions/support/`.

Expense

Zoho Expense is an affordable and effective way to get your team expense management in order.

You can upload receipts for your daily business expenses on the go via a native mobile app, which is quite handy for business travelers. Employees can create expense reports by entering receipts and importing card transactions, and then submitting the expense reports for approval and reimbursement. Accounts will love this way of receiving clear and structured information.

You can connect Zoho Expense to Zoho Books, Invoice, and CRM, as well as QuickBooks and Slack (for notifications).

■ **Reference**   To learn more about Zoho Expense, check out `https://www.zoho.com/expense/support/`.

Inventory

Zoho Inventory offers an easy-to-use and cost-effective inventory and order-management solution in the cloud. Using Inventory, you can create and manage sales and purchase orders, keep track of available stock, and get real-time reports on your logistics operation. All of these are possible while you work from your office or on the go via the Inventory mobile app.

Zoho Inventory offers integration with shipping services, such as FedEx, UPS, and DHL; online stores such as Amazon, eBay, Etsy, and Shopify; as well as other Zoho apps such as Books and CRM.

If you manage a small inventory and shipping operation out of a single warehouse, you can give Zoho Inventory a try for free. As your business grows, you can opt for a suitable paid edition and manage tens of thousands of orders per month in multiple warehouses.

■ **Reference**   To learn more about Zoho Inventory, check out `https://www.zoho.com/inventory/support/`.

IT and Help Desk Apps

Zoho's IT apps will help organizations that need IT support tools to streamline their processes and stay productive. Four apps (as of spring 2017) will help your IT team provide online and remote support, and manage IT issues and mobile devices.

Desk

Per Zoho, Desk is the "industry's first context-aware help desk software."

Customer-centricity must be at the core of every business, and not degraded to merely a fluffy statement in marketing campaigns. Customer experience actually starts before customers buy your products or services and continues as long as the customers use them.

Zoho Desk tries to improve the often underwhelming (or worse) experience of dealing with help desks. Apart from standard issue tracking and ticket management tools, Desk offers a centralized, focused, and contextual interface to support teams to stay on top of the tasks in hand and manage incoming inquiries from various channels, such as phone and email, efficiently.

Zoho Desk also allows you to create a customer service portal and knowledge base for your customers, from which they can find solutions to common problems, or file and manage their tickets to new issues.

Detailed reporting, a mobile app for customer service on the go, and integration with other Zoho apps such as CRM and Projects is also available out of the box.

Even if you are a tiny operation, customer service should still be a key aspect of your business culture. That's how you get loyal customers, repeat business, and referrals.

■ **Reference**   To learn more about Zoho Desk, check out `https://www.zoho.com/desk/help/`.

Assist

Zoho Assist provides an easy way to remotely access computers inside and outside your organization for tech support and troubleshooting.

Zoho Assist is a great tool if you need to show a customer how to do a certain task, or better, do it for them remotely while they are watching (and hopefully learning). You can save time and money and most possibly reduce your carbon footprint by minimizing site visits for trivial troubleshooting tasks.

With Zoho Assist you can also remotely access unattended computers (needs software installed), so you don't need someone on the other side to give you access. You can transfer files, reboot devices remotely, and access multiple monitors on the host machines.

You can start using Zoho Assist for free for basic tasks, so nothing stands between you and helping your clients, colleagues, or your mom remotely with troubleshooting tasks. Now you can help her bring back that document that magically disappeared from her desktop.

■ **Reference**   To learn more about Zoho Assist, check out `https://www.zoho.com/ assist/resources.html`.

ServiceDesk Plus

For serious IT support, Zoho offers ServiceDesk Plus On-Demand from ManageEngine (IT management division of Zoho). It allows you to track and manage IT tickets, resolve issues, and maximize end-user satisfaction.

With ServiceDesk Plus, you have various automation options at your disposal, self-service portal, out-of-the-box ITIL (Information Technology Infrastructure Library) workflows, SLA (service Level Agreement) creation, and a host of other features to ensure successful service desk operation for your business.

■ **Reference**   To learn more about Zoho ServiceDesk Plus, check out https://ondemand. manageengine.com/service-desk/support.html.

Mobile Device Management

If you need enterprise-level mobile device management for your organization, then Mobile Device Manager Plus could be for you. Offered by ManageEngine, the IT division of Zoho, Mobile Device Manager Plus lets you set up, supervise, and secure your enterprise mobile devices and apps.

■ **Reference**   To learn more about Zoho Mobile Device Management, check out https://www.manageengine.com/mobile-device-management/support.html.

Human Resources Apps

It is argued that people are a company's greatest asset. Whether you agree with this statement or not, it is important to ensure human resource operations are managed properly at all times.

Zoho offers two powerful apps for small to medium businesses (SMBs) to manage recruiting fresh blood and also smoothly manage the existing workforce.

Recruit

Zoho Recruit is a cloud-based recruitment solution for recruiting agencies and corporate HR (Human Resources) departments. You can create and manage job postings, publish them on company websites as well as job boards such as Monster and Indeed, parse resumes, manage candidates and communications, and automate tedious HR tasks with workflows.

There is a mobile app for HR ninjas and a free edition for you to give applicant tracking and interview scheduling features a try.

■ **Reference**   To learn more about Zoho Recruit, check out https://www.zoho.com/recruit/resources.html.

People

As you grow, your team grows too. Usually the moment you pass five employees, HR requirements, if not handled properly, start to impact productivity and other business processes. So, considering an HR solution early on may be a prudent way to go forward.

On the other hand, for companies larger than 5-10 employees, in-house or outsourced HR management will become a necessity.

Zoho People is a cloud-based HR management service, which helps you manage all HR-related tasks without losing your mind to needy employees. You can manage employee information securely, provide self-service features for managers and staff, perform time tracking and attendance, and create performance reviews and other important reports about your people.

You can start for free to manage up to five employees with Zoho People. Then as you hire more people, possibly through Zoho Recruit, you can upgrade to paid plans and utilize all the features that People provides in your HR processes.

■ **Reference**   To learn more about Zoho People, check out https://www.zoho.com/people/help/home.html.

Where to Start

As you saw in this chapter, Zoho offers a dizzying list of apps. Most of these apps work beautifully together and help you streamline your business and stay more productive.

Some of these apps have overlapping features, and it may be confusing which one to choose if you are just starting with Zoho or are new to SaaS. So, I try and give a number of recommendations in order, which I believe would be applicable to many small businesses:

- No matter if you are a solopreneur, a freelancer, or an organization of one thousand employees, start with Zoho CRM. Make CRM a part of your day-to-day business process as well as long-term growth plans. The free edition is a great place to get started. In this book, I will cover in detail how to best utilize CRM and make it work for your business.

- Become more productive by moving your emails to Zoho Mail for better integration with CRM. Although CRM offers integration with Google Apps and Microsoft Outlook, nothing beats native compatibility between Zoho apps. One big bonus here is that you can host up to 25 users on Mail for free, and that is with your own custom domain.

- Incorporate Zoho Campaigns as soon as you can. Almost no business, no matter how small, can ignore digital marketing. A big part of digital marketing is email and social marketing and Zoho Campaign will help you win big here.

- Get serious about accounting and use either of Zoho Expense, Zoho Invoice, or Zoho Books, depending on the size of your operation.

- Zoho Projects should be another key part of your cloud suite. With great integration with CRM and Books, you can easily stay on top of your projects and manage the operation of your team more effectively.

- When your team grows and requirements become more complex, use Zoho Creator and Zoho Reports for more advanced business processes and adapt Zoho Recruit and People to manage human resources.

Once you have these apps utilized, you will see how streamlined your processes will become and how much time and money you will be saving. Your team and your customers will be happier, which means you will be happier too.

Summary

In this chapter, we had a bird's eye view of the Zoho suite. I hope you see how interconnected Zoho suite apps are and how using as many Zoho apps as possible in your business will improve productivity and save you time and money.

In the next chapter, we will look at how CRM as a practice, and not a mere software solution, is a key factor to the success of your business. We will also get introduced to some basic business-process management concepts to guide us throughout this book.

CHAPTER 2

■ ■ ■

CRM at Your Business Core

This chapter, as daunting as it may look, is arguably one of the most important chapters in this book. Before jumping right into the exciting stuff and starting to explore Zoho CRM, let's take a step back and review what makes a CRM implementation successful.

If concepts, such as CRM, business process, or process modeling are new to you, treat yourself to a double espresso (or your favorite hot drink), read through this chapter, and study the references provided as well. I promise to stay as shallow as possible and yet provide you with enough information to get you going.

On the other hand, if you already have your processes mapped (and possibly improved), or you can map processes with your eyes closed, feel free to skip this chapter.

The Why, the What, and the How

It is easy and perilous to get distracted by the fancy shiny IT world and forget *what* you are trying to achieve; *how* you want to achieve it; and most importantly, *why* you want to achieve it anyway. Let's put this into perspective.

For instance, imagine you want to implement a CRM for your organization. After all, it is most probably why you are reading this book, instead of sipping a piña colada at the beach.

Now let's revisit the definition of CRM:

> *CRM is a management philosophy according to which a company's goals can be best achieved through identification and satisfaction of the customers' stated and unstated needs and wants.*

So it is safe to say that *what* you want to achieve is to make your customers happy.

Why you want happy customers has obviously something to do with wanting more business and hopefully more money in your bank account.

How you achieve this lofty goal, on the other hand, is by implementing a CRM in your organization.

Why am I taking your precious time by garbling philosophy, you ask? To ask you to take a step back and make sure a CRM is the right tool for you to achieve your goals. By reaching this level of conviction about the means to achieve your organizational goals, you will be able to design the best solution that addresses every single business requirement and improves efficiency and effectiveness of your efforts in keeping the customers happy and your business profitable.

© Ali Shabdar 2017

A. Shabdar, *Mastering Zoho CRM*, DOI 10.1007/978-1-4842-2904-0_2

CRM

According to the Oxford dictionary,[1] CRM stands for Customer Relationship Management and denotes strategies and software that enable a company to optimize its customer relations.

BusinessDictionary, on the other hand, gives two detailed and clearer definitions:[2]

1. A management philosophy according to which a company's goals can be best achieved through identification and satisfaction of the customers' stated and unstated needs and wants.

2. A computerized system for identifying, targeting, acquiring, and retaining the best mix of customers.

Customer relationship management helps in profiling prospects, understanding their needs, and in building relationships with them by providing the most suitable products and enhanced customer service. It integrates back and front office systems to create a database of customer contacts, purchases, and technical support, among other things. This database helps the company in presenting a unified face to its customers, and improve the quality of the relationship, while enabling customers to manage some information on their own.

I particularly like how the definition emphasizes that CRM, first and foremost, is a management philosophy. The reason I obsess with this statement is that in many cases, when an organization implements an information system, such as CRM, the software is deemed a magic wand that you point at the mess you are in, and voilà! It solves all your problems.

The reality is quite the opposite. Throwing software in the mix of organizational chaos usually leads to more chaos and frustration. It is surprising that even large enterprises that do due diligence and have all the complex IT models and methods at their disposal fall in this trap too.

As a small business you cannot afford to make such mistakes, especially since you have way less resources to gamble with. Although cloud computing and SaaS saves you thousands of dollars in upfront IT, implementing information systems needs expensive resources, such as time, and it could increase business risk in the transition period.

By utilizing a CRM you take control of three main aspects of your business operation (Figure 2-1):

- Marketing

- Sales

- Customer service

---

[1] https://en.oxforddictionaries.com/definition/crm
[2] http://www.businessdictionary.com/definition/customer-relationship-management-CRM.html

Figure 2-1. *CRM loop*

Customer relationship management is a perpetual loop. The longer you can keep a client in this loop, the more they become and the more successful you are. Your CRM must model this loop effectively and help you win new customers while retaining loyal customers for the foreseeable future.

In this book you will see how to set up Zoho CRM and utilize its power to do exactly that.

Beyond CRM

Before we go any further, it is worth mentioning Enterprise Resource Planning (ERP) and Business Process Management (BPM) in here. Both are very important in the business world, and many books and courses are available on both topics.

ERP

The next level for a business using CRM properly is to consider implementing an ERP system and integrating it with your CRM. ERP brings additional activities of an organization, such as finance, supply chain, human resources, and reporting under one roof to be integrated and managed effectively.

There are many enterprise-level ERP systems, such as SAP ERP, Oracle ERP Cloud, and Microsoft Dynamics ERP.

However, for small businesses and solopreneurs, ERP is overkill. Simply start with a robust CRM, such as (Zoho) CRM and as your requirements grow, incorporate Zoho Books, Zoho People, Zoho Inventory, Zoho Projects, Zoho Reports, and other tools to create your customized and effective mini ERP.

BPM

According to BusinessDictionary,[3] BPM is an activity undertaken by businesses to identify, evaluate, and improve business processes. With the advancement of technology, BPM can now be effectively managed with software that is customized based on the metrics and policies specified by a company. This type of action is essential to businesses seeking to improve process performance-related issues so that they can better serve their clients.

■ **Reference**   To get a better idea of what BPM is, read Nathaniel Palmer's post.[4]

BPM is quite enterprise focused and in large organizations systems such as ERP and CRM could very well be a part of a much larger enterprise BPM.

We won't be talking about BPM in here beyond a mere honorable mention. What we will focus on, however, is the practice of mapping business processes and then using it quite lightly to design our CRM implementation properly.

But before that, let's understand what we mean by business processes.

Process, Process, Process

Everything in this seemingly infinite world is a part of a process. It is hard to argue with this statement. After all, a process is a series of actions or steps taken in order to achieve a particular end.

Even the simplest, most mundane things in our daily lives involve multiple processes. When you wake up in the morning and make yourself a cup of coffee, you take part in a complex process with underlying subprocesses. Some of these subprocesses are a trip to the kitchen, preparing coffee, and consuming it.

Let's break down the trip to the kitchen:

1. Gently get out of the bed:

    a. don't wake up the angel (or demon) sleeping next to you.

2. Walk toward the door.

3. If the bedroom door is closed:

    a. open the bedroom door,

    b. close the door behind you,

    c. pass through the door.

4. If the bedroom door is open:

    a. pass through the door.

---

[3] http://www.businessdictionary.com/definition/business-process-management-BPM.html
[4] http://bpm.com/what-is-bpm

5. Walk across the hall.

6. Avoid stepping on the cat purring right in the middle of the hall.

7. Arrive in the kitchen.

I bet you can add or change a few steps depending on your own coffee-making routine. Now, if you were the obsessive type, you would have wanted to map every single step of this process and see whether there is room for improvement. For instance, what if you always kept the door open, or would it help if you installed an automatic sliding door for the bedroom?

It may seem excessive, or downright ridiculous, to install an automatic sliding bedroom door only to skip two steps in your morning coffee ritual. However, in a business scenario – where efficiency is important – the scale of things changes dramatically.

Imagine a good old door installed on the way to the kitchen in a busy restaurant. If, on average, 3 staff members were to pass through that door every 5 minutes during a normal 8 hour shift, the poor door would need to open and close 288 times every single day. Considering maintenance costs, hygiene, and safety measures, an automatic kitchen door for a restaurant may not be a bad idea, after all.

You can find similar examples in your work environment. Virtually, any business process can be improved. But before improving a process, first we need to fully understand it.

Map All Processes

An effective way of understanding all aspects of an existing process is to create a visual representation of it, that is, map it.

Mapping business processes also helps to make sure when implementing information systems (e.g., CRM), the behavior and outcome of such systems match, complement, and improve the existing processes.

Example: Imagine, up until a week ago, your sales team relied on Gmail and Microsoft Excel to manage their clients and deals. It was certainly less than ideal, but it was working nonetheless.

Then, you roll out a new CRM to manage the sales force and to improve efficiency across the board. Since you are a smart and caring manager (or consultant), you make sure staff goes through a full CRM training before the launch, so the transition from Gmail/Excel to CRM is as smooth as possible.

You make it clear that after the new CRM is implemented, all data is to be centralized, and keeping information on scattered Excel sheets is considered heresy. Everything is going smoothly and all heads are in constant nodding mode in team meetings.

Then the disaster strikes. Two days after the launch of the CRM, your new dream world comes down crumbling because a workflow in the CRM that automates sending emails to the reporting managers skips an internal approval process and messes up the whole chain of command. Oh, boy.

Three days and a few unpleasant meetings later, you find out that the process in question was not mapped properly nor it was signed off by the management prior to being implemented in the CRM.

Unfortunately, incidents such as the just mentioned are not as isolated as one could wish for. After all, human error is a part of the job, but it can be minimized with a few steps taken in the right direction, that is, mapping, analyzing, and signing off all business processes prior to even choosing an information solution.

How to Map Processes

According to Nathaniel Palmer, business process mapping is to "identify, define, and make a representation of the complete process to support communication about the process. There is no single standard way to model, but the model must encompass the process."

It is worth mentioning that process modeling, in contrast to process mapping, is focused on the optimization of the processes, which happens after they are properly mapped.

It is a good idea to learn process mapping according to industry standards and best practices to make sure other professionals understand it and can continue your work without going back to square one. One of these standards is BPMN.

BPMN

A common standard for modeling business processes is BPMN (Business Process Model and Notation).[5] Figure 2-2 is an example of a very simple process map representing the steps and logical connections of processing an order in a typical scenario.

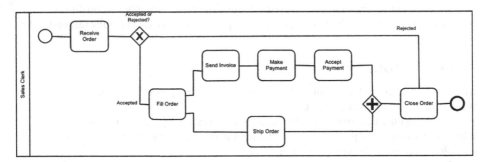

Figure 2-2. *A process map*

■ **Reference**   The process model in Figure 2-2 was downloaded from Business Process Incubator.[6] Business Process Incubator is a great place to start your journey as business owner or consultant in the world of business process management. Make sure you keep their BPMN quick guide[7] handy when mapping processes.

Tools of the Trade

As you can expect, there is a myriad of process mapping and modeling tools available out there. Most of these tools are targeted to enterprise users, but we are going to stick to simpler, more affordable options, which can do exactly what we need: to turn mysterious business processes and procedures into clear and readable visual diagrams.

---

[5]http://www.bpmn.org/
[6]https://www.businessprocessincubator.com/content/order-processing/
[7]http://www.bpmnquickguide.com/viewit.html

You can use any diagramming tool, such as the all capable Microsoft Visio, or the versatile and cloud-based LucidChart. Each one of these tools offers the essentials of modeling and has unique features to address the requirements of different users.

Microsoft Visio, for example, is very common among the enterprise users who use Microsoft ERP and CRM solutions. Visio is also quite similar to Microsoft Office applications in terms of look and feel. This familiar interface makes it easier for experienced Office users to pick up Visio faster.

LucidChart, on the other hand, is lightweight, suitable for a variety of scenarios, and offers different monthly subscription options for different requirements.

In this book we are going to use the nifty Camunda Modeler[8] to map our business processes based on the BPMN 2.0 industry standard. This is quite handy and future proof as you can use the maps created with Camunda Modeler directly for process modeling and improvement in the future.

You can install Camunda Modeler on Mac, Windows, and GNU/Linux, or simply run it on Chrome.

■ **Note**   To learn how to install Camunda Modeler on your system, refer to the installation guide at `https://docs.camunda.org/manual/7.6/installation/camunda-modeler/`.

In Figure 2-3 you can see Camunda Modeler (version 1.5.1) in action, with the same model from Figure 2-2 loaded in to the modeler.

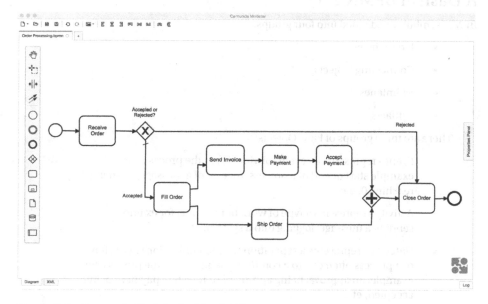

Figure 2-3. *Camunda Modeler for Mac 1.5.1*

---

[8]`https://camunda.org/bpmn/tool/`

You can edit, print, and export this model. Click on one of the objects (symbols) on the map and a context menu will appear (Figure 2-4). You can also perform a number of actions such as editing or removing the object, or adding new objects to the map.

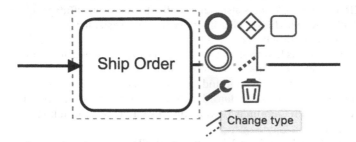

Figure 2-4. *Object context menu*

Getting Started with Process Mapping

In this section, we will create a very simple process map with Camunda Modeler to learn the basics of process mapping. Let's start by learning the most basic BPMN symbols.

A Dash of BPMN 2.0

BPMN symbols are divided into four groups:

- Flow Objects

- Connecting Objects

- Swimlanes

- Artifacts

There are three groups of Flow Objects:

- Event - represents an event (obviously) in the process, for example start or end of a process, receipt of a message, a timer reaching 0, etc.

- Activity - represents a type of work being done, for example, sending a message, logging into a system, etc.

- Gateway - represents a separation (or recombination) in the flow of a process often due to a condition being met in the process, for example, an approval being approved or rejected, payment being accepted, etc.

Connecting Objects connect the flow objects showing a sequence of actions, the route of a message from one stage (or participant to another), or the relationship between flow objects (Figure 2-5). These objects are shown as arrowed lines.

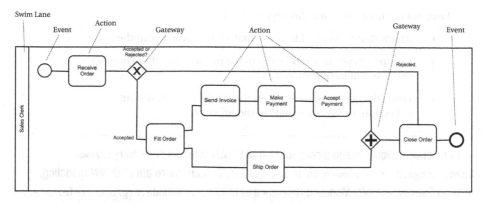

Figure 2-5. *BPMN symbols*

In Figure 2-6 you notice a container box labeled as Sales Clerk. This box is called a Swimlane (or Lane, for brevity). Lanes are used to group other objects (symbols) and separate logical or actual aspects of a process. Not surprisingly, a collection of lanes is called a Pool.

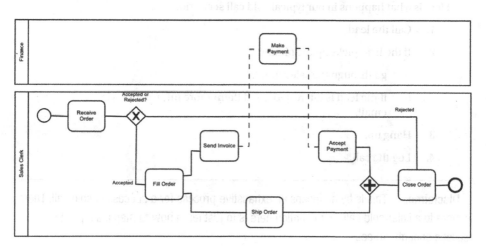

Figure 2-6. *Swimlanes*

For example, when processing orders in an organization, the order is initially received by the Sales department. After going through a few steps, the order is submitted to the Finance department for some accounting work, and then is sent back to Sales for further processing.

To show this interdepartmental flow, process steps are placed in two adjacent lanes called Sales and Finance to show which steps happen where. This not only helps clarify the flow, but also it could reveal interdependencies and possible inefficiencies caused by a delay in the Finance department. There, you discovered a bottleneck in the process.

Last, but not least, there are three types of Artifacts:

- Annotations - to provide additional information about the map;

- Groups - to put tasks and parts of the process together showing some sort of significance; and

- Data Objects - to represent presence of data input, output, collection, or storage of data in the process.

■ **Reference**   You can see a complete list of BPMN symbols here: `http://www.bpmnquickguide.com/view-bpmn-quick-guide/`. To learn more about BPMN modeling, head to Camunda BPMN Modeling Reference at `https://camunda.org/bpmn/reference/`.

Your First Process Map

To get our hands dirty, we are going to map a very simple process: cold calling procedure for a local insurance broker.

Here is what happens in our typical cold call scenario:

1. Call the lead.

2. If the lead picks up the phone:

    a.   go through the sales script.

    b.   if the lead is interested, send them more information via email.

3. Hang up.

4. Log the call.

■ **Disclaimer**   This is by no means an exhaustive process for a successful cold call. There is more to a killer cold call. Our intention here is to just learn how to map a simple, but realistic enough, process.

EXERCISE 1 – COLD CALLING PROCESS MAP

Follow these steps to map the above process:

1.   Open Camunda Modeler (Figure 2-7).

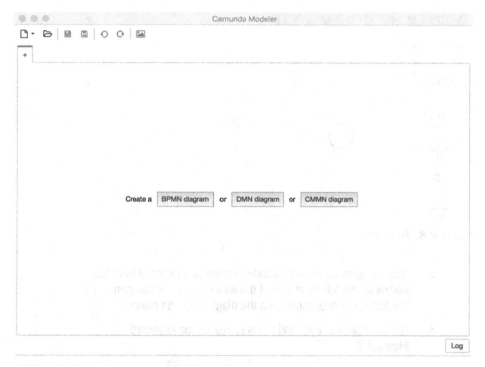

Figure 2-7. *Camunda Modeler for Mac, version 1.5.1*

2. Click *Create a BPMN diagram* button in the middle of the main window, or press Command+T (on Mac), or Windows+T (on Windows) on your keyboard. A new diagram will open with an *Event* symbol (circle) placed in it. This symbol indicates the start of the process (Figure 2-8).

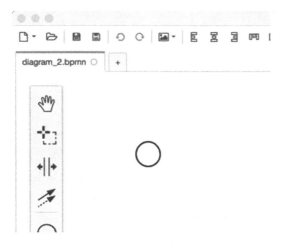

Figure 2-8. *Start symbol*

3. Drag and drop an *Activity* (rounded rectangular) symbol from the toolbox on the left-hand side of the window into the diagram. The Activity symbol appears on the diagram in edit mode.

4. Type in *"Call the Lead"* and press Enter on the keyboard (Figure 2-9).

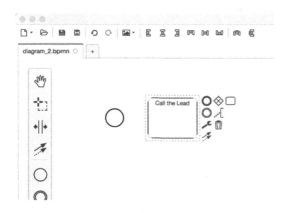

Figure 2-9. *Activity symbol*

5. Click the *Start Event* symbol (circle) and on the context menu click on the arrows icons (Figure 2-10). A dashed line appears connected to the mouse cursor.

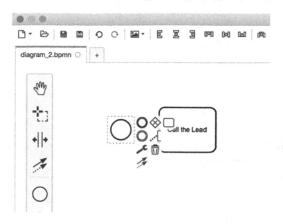

Figure 2-10. *Symbol context menu*

6. Move the cursor toward the Activity symbol until the cursor touches the left side of the rectangular shape. The color of the rectangle turns light green (Figure 2-11).

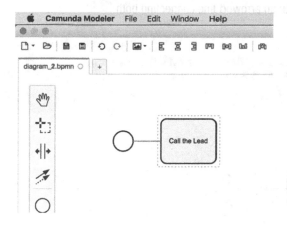

Figure 2-11. *Connecting symbols*

7. Click again. An arrowed line will be placed between the two symbols connecting them. Then a context menu appears automatically ready for you to pick the next symbol that is connected to the *"Call the Lead"* Activity (Figure 2-12).

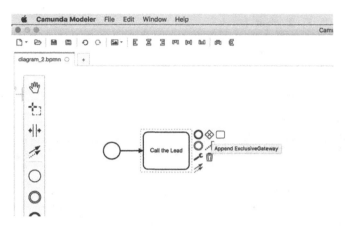

Figure 2-12. *Ready for the next symbol*

8. In the context menu, click on the *Gateway* symbol. A moving shape appears. Move the cursor until the shape is aligned with the other symbols and click again. A Gateway shape will be placed on the diagram with an arrowed line connecting both symbols (Figure 2-13).

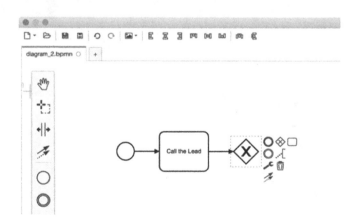

Figure 2-13. *Gateway symbol*

9. Label the Gateway symbol as *"Lead Picks up the Phone?"*

10. Add an Activity symbol labeled *"Go Through the Sales Script"* (Figure 2-14).

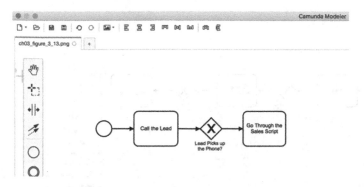

Figure 2-14. *Adding another activity symbol*

11. Add a Gateway symbol labeled *"Lead Interested?"*

12. Label the line connecting the previous Gateway and Activity symbols *"Yes"* (Figure 2-15).

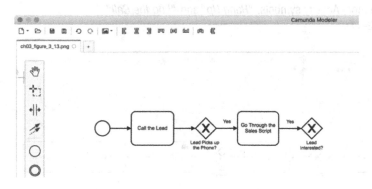

Figure 2-15. *Adding another gateway symbol*

13. Add another Activity and label *"Email Information."*

14. **Bonus:** Click on the symbol and select the tool icon in the context menu. A drop-down menu appears to select the Activity type.

35

15. Select *"Send Task"* in the drop-down menu. A mail icon appears in the Activity symbol (Figure 2-16).

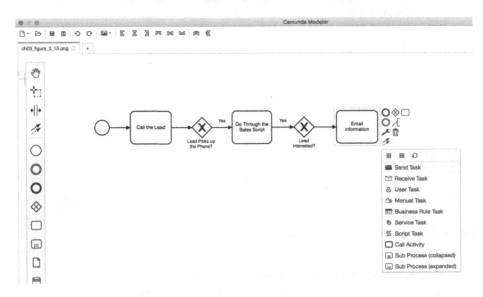

Figure 2-16. *Specifiying activity type as a send task*

16. Add two more Activity symbols: *"Hang Up"* and *"Log the Call"* (Figure 2-17).

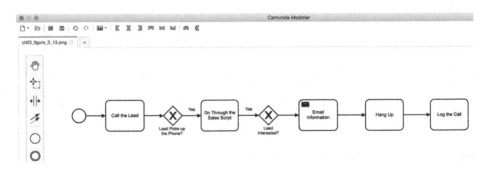

Figure 2-17. *Adding final activities*

17. Then add an *End Event* to indicate the end of the process
     (Figure 2-18). There are still two steps missing from the process
     map.

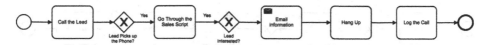

Figure 2-18. *Adding the end event symbol*

18. Click the *"Lead Picks Up the Phone?"* Gateway symbol and
     select the arrowed line icon in the context menu. Then move the
     cursor and drop it on the *"Hang Up"* Activity.

19. A line connects the two symbols but overlaps other symbols on
     the way. Fix it by hovering the cursor on the arrowed line and
     clicking when a yellow dot appears on the line (Figure 2-19).

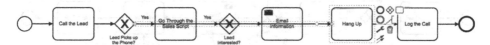

Figure 2-19. *Fixing the overlapping arrowed line, step 1*

20. Then click and drag the line away until a broken line is created
     (Figure 2-20).

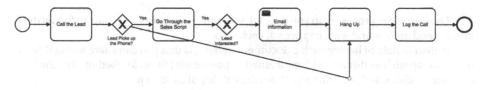

Figure 2-20. *Fixing the overlapping arrowed line, step 2*

21. Repeat the same on the left side of the line and create a parallel connection between the Gateway and the activity shapes (Figure 2-21).

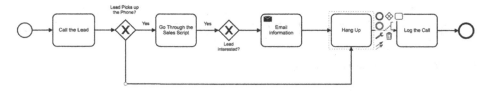

Figure 2-21. *Fixing the overlapping arrowed line, step 2*

22. Similarly connect the *"Lead Interested?"* Gateway to *"Hang Up"* Activity and finish the process map (Figure 2-22).

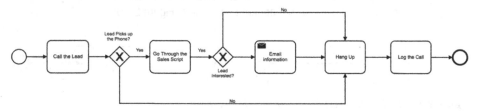

Figure 2-22. *Final process map*

Congratulations! You mapped your first business process.

Looking at the process map you created, you can see how easy it is now to follow the process and understand what happens at each step.

A great benefit of having such a document in hand is that you can share a readable process map such as this one with concerned departments (Sales, Marketing, etc.) and get their feedback and confirmation about the validity of each step.

Summary

In this chapter, you learned, albeit very lightly, about a number of foundational concepts, such as CRM, ERP, and BPM. We discussed that the key to implementing a successful CRM is to understand exactly what we intend to do and why we are doing it in the first place.

We also had a quick look at process mapping and how it can save you time and money before you embark on implementing any information solution, including a CRM.

I hope I could trigger the interest in you to learn more about process analysis and understating how your business works on a granular level. By looking closer into day-to-day operations, you will be surprised to learn about steps or connections that you didn't know existed, or the unknown bottlenecks that impacted the efficiency of your business.

In the next chapter, we will start using Zoho CRM and prepare it for prime time.

CHAPTER 3

■ ■ ■

Getting Started with Zoho CRM

In the previous chapter, we had a quick look at how a CRM system (Zoho CRM, here) can be, and frankly, should be at the core of your business. We also learned about the very basics of how to understand and map your business processes.

By mapping your processes accurately, you will have a clear idea of how the day-to-day operations of your business improve or impede productivity and efficiency throughout your business. You can then begin to improve them.

Additionally, for our purpose, which is to set up a solid CRM system from ground up, these process maps will help replicate the exact processes in the CRM.

For example, the specific way your sales funnel (pipeline) is designed needs to be reflected in the CRM. These include actions taken by the salespeople from start to finish, the documents created and submitted in the process, approvals, notifications, emails, and workflows.

Imagine a world in which you have eliminated unnecessary paper trails and automated trivial tasks, such as submitting documents for approval. A lot of these inefficient processes can be replicated and automated in the CRM. Just don't expect CRM to do everything for you. You may still need HR systems, inventory systems, and project management tools; however, CRM will take care of the heart of your business, that is, sales, and communicate with other tools and systems improving productivity even more.

With all the preparation and appreciation of the philosophy of CRM under our belt, you are now ready to start working on Zoho CRM and learn how to build exactly what your business needs.

Getting Started

To start with Zoho CRM, open your favorite browser (Chrome, Safari, Firefox, Edge, etc.) and log onto https://crm.zoho.com/.

I will assume that this is your first time here, so before we do anything else, we will need to create an account. This account is a universal Zoho account and you can use it to access other Zoho services, such as Mail, Campaigns, Books, etc.

© Ali Shabdar 2017

A. Shabdar, *Mastering Zoho CRM*, DOI 10.1007/978-1-4842-2904-0_3

To create a new Zoho account, follow these steps:

1. On the homepage (Figure 3-1), type in your name, email, and a strong password.

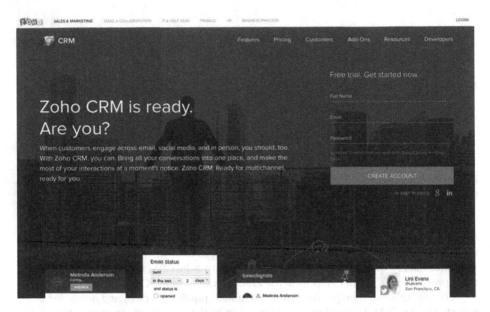

***Figure 3-1.** Zoho CRM homepage*

■ **Note** Building strong passwords for all your accounts, especially accounts in which you keep confidential business information, is paramount. You can use tools, such as Keychain Access for Mac OS, lastPass,[1] or Zoho Vault[2] to create and manage strong passwords for your accounts.

---

2. Click on the *Create Account* button to initiate the sign-up process. Within moments, you will receive a confirmation email from Zoho asking you to confirm your email address.

3. Click *Confirm your account* button in the email. Upon successful confirmation, you will be redirected to the login page.

4. In the login page, enter your email address and the password you chose in step 1 and then click *Login*.

---

[1]https://lastpass.com/
[2]https://www.zoho.com/vault/

5. In the next page, you will be asked to enable Two Factor
    Authentication (TFA) (Figure 3-2). I strongly suggest you enable
    this feature as it will dramatically improve the security level
    of your account against possible attacks (hacking, etc.). Click
    Set up to Protect Now and follow the onscreen instructions to
    enable TFA. If you want to do this later, you can click the link
    below the button that reads *Skip Two Factor Authentication*.

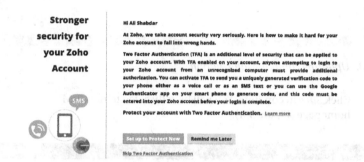

Figure 3-2. *Enabling Two Factor Authentication*

■ **What is Two Factor Authentication?** Two Factor Authentication adds an extra layer of
security to your account. Once enabled, Sign-In will require you to enter a unique verification
code generated by an app on your mobile device or sent via text message, in addition to
your username and password.

If you opted not to enable this feature during the first setup, you can always enable it at
`https://accounts.zoho.com/u/h#security/authentication`.

---

6. In the next page, you will be asked to update your company
    information. Enter relevant information for the following
    (Figure 3-3):

    a. Company Name

    b. Phone Number

    c. Mobile Number

    d. Time Zone (of your headquarters)

    e. Language

    f. Currency Locale

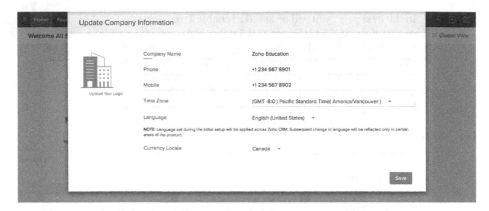

Figure 3-3. Updating company information

7. Click *Save* to continue. You will be redirected to the CRM homepage (Figure 3-4).

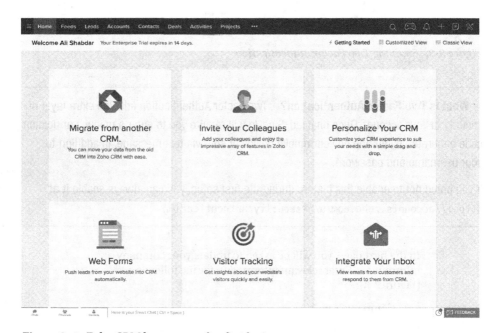

Figure 3-4. Zoho CRM homepage after first login

Quick Tour of the Homepage

On the homepage (Figure 3-4), you'll be greeted by six big buttons, each helping you get started with the CRM. We will skip these fancy buttons.

On top of the page, there is a menu bar with items such as Home, Feeds, Leads, etc. Each one of these menus items loads a CRM module (more on this later).

On the right-hand side of the menu bar, there are six buttons that allow you to access other features of the CRM, such as set up, messages, and calendar.

Below the menu bar, there is a contextual bar with a welcome message on the left side and three items on the right to switch between different views of the homepage:

- Getting Started (the current view,)

- Customized View, and

- Classic View.

Go ahead and switch between them. There is not much to see now, but after data is entered into CRM and with some cusomiztion, you can view the current state of your business right in your homepage.

Right next to the welcome message is a message in red warning you that you have 14 days until your Enterprise trial expires. By default, all new Zoho CRM accounts come for a limited time with all the features enabled for users to test all aspects of CRM and then choose the edition they need. You can ignore this for now.

■ **Reminder**   Zoho CRM comes in four different editions: Free, Standard, Professional, and Enterprise Edition.

Each one of these editions comes with a different set of features and capabilities with the Free edition being the most basic and the Enterprise edition the most advanced one in the mix. As a courtesy (and a way of trying all the features), Zoho gives new users a 14-day trial of the Enterprise edition. After this period your account will revert to the Free edition. The Free edition is quite capable for small operations; however, you may need one of the paid editions as per your business requirements.

Learn more about all the features available to different editions of CRM here: https://www.zoho.com/crm/help/erutaef321.html.

CRM Terminology

The key to effectively managing the sales processes of your organization is to know exactly in what stage of the pipeline (or sales funnel) a potential customer or a deal is. CRM manages the entire pipeline in a central location, automates many mundane processes, and improves the productivity and efficiency of the sales force.

In a typical (sales-focused) business environment, terms such as lead, prospect, customer, opportunity, validation, account etc. is commonplace. Naturally, CRM systems adopt such terms in their terminology and Zoho CRM is no exception.

Below are four of the key terms used in Zoho CRM:

- **Lead** – A lead is an unqualified contact or sales opportunity. For example, the business cards collected in an exhibition, or a cold referral received from a partner is a lead. Leads enter the sales pipeline from early stages and need to be qualified (validated) via follow-ups and other methods.

- **Contact** – Once a lead is qualified it gets *converted* in the CRM. One output of this conversion is a Contact who is a person with whom you interact during a sales process. For example, suppose you are trying to sell raw material to a company overseas. You have found and contacted the procurement manager who happens to be interested in listening to your offer. This person become a contact.

- **Deal** – When you qualify (convert) a lead, it generates asecond output, which is the potential deal between you and your client. This is called a Deal and goes through various stages in the pipeline.

- **Account** – Finally, the last outcome of converting a lead is an Account, which is a company or a department within a company that you do business with. Each account can have one more Contacts assigned to it.

■ **Note** You can create contacts, deals, or accounts directly without taking them through the lead conversion process. This is particularly useful when you work with exitisng contact, deals, or accounts and just want to import them as they are into the CRM.

There is more to CRM terminologies. We will learn about teach one as we use them in the upcoming chapters. For a list of all terminologies, refer to Zoho Help:

`https://www.zoho.com/crm/help/understanding-zohocrm.html#Terminologies`

CRM Modules

Zoho CRM categorizes data into logical groups based on their type of content. These groups are called modules and each come with a set of unique features relevant to the information they manage.

Here is the complete list of standard Zoho CRM modules grouped by their type of operation:

- Sales Force Automation

  - Leads

  - Accounts

- Contacts
- Deals (or Opportunities, formerly known as Potentials)
- Forecasts
- Marketing Automation
  - Campaigns
- Customer Support
  - Cases
  - Solutions
- Inventory Management
  - Products
  - Vendors
  - Sales Quotes
  - Purchase Orders
  - Sales Orders
  - Invoices
  - Price Books
- Data Analytics
  - Reports
  - Dashboards
- Activities
  - Tasks
  - Events
  - Call Logs

The name of each module is quite self-explanatory and each represents a common business process used by majority of the organizations. We will be using most of these modules in various contexts and learn more about inner workings of each one as we go forward.

These modules work together seamlessly addressing almost all requiremnts of a typical business operation. That said, you can customize them as per your business requirements and make them work better for you.

On the other hand, if you have a drastically different set of requirements, you have the option to create custom modules. For example, for a real estate company, you can customize the Products module to maintin your listings, or create a Listings module from scratch and use Products for other purposes.

Setting Up Zoho CRM

CRM has a powerful Setup page in which you can customize its many features. We will be visiting the Setup page often, but for now we simply need to modify some general settings, namely:

- Personal Settings

- Company Details

- Users

- Email Settings

Follow these steps to configure the general settings:

1. On the top right of the page, in the menu bar, click on the tools button and select *Setup* in the context menu (Figure 3-5). Setup page opens (Figure 3-6).

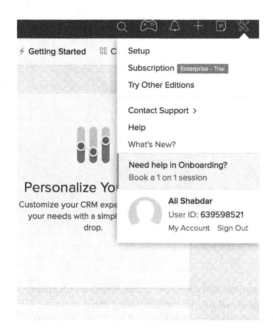

Figure 3-5. *Tools context menu*

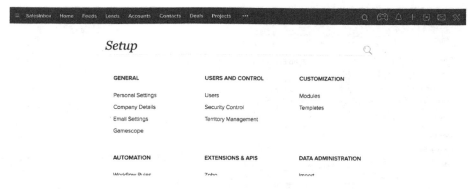

Figure 3-6. *CRM Setup page*

2. In the Setup page, under *GENERAL* group, click *Personal Settings*. Personal settings page opens.

3. Click on the small pen icon next to each field and edit the values (Figure 3-7).

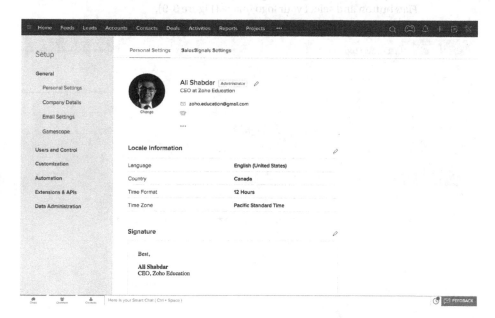

Figure 3-7. *Personal Settings page*

4. Next, click on *Company Details* on the left sidebar. *Company Detail* will open (Figure 3-8).

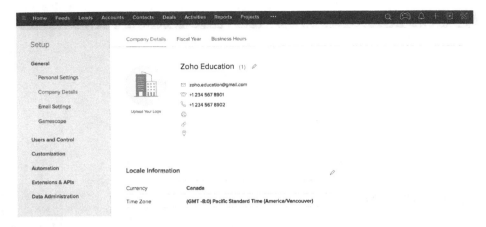

Figure 3-8. Company Details page

5. Click the *Upload Your Logo* link under the logo placeholder.

6. In the *Upload Your Logo* dialog box, click the *Browse Local Files* button and select your logo image (Figure 3-9).

Figure 3-9. Uploading company logo

7. Click the pen icon next to company name. The *Company Details* dialog box will open.

8. In the *Company Details* box, enter your company information and click *Save* when you are done (Figure 3-10).

Figure 3-10. *Editing company details*

9. On top of the *Company Details* page, click the *Fiscal Year* tab.

10. In the *Fiscal Year* tab, change the month in *Fiscal year begins* drop-down, if January (default value) is not the start of the fiscal year for your organization and click *Save* to apply the change (Figure 3-11).

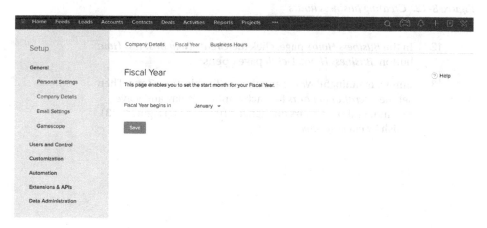

Figure 3-11. *Setting fiscal year*

11. Next, select the *Business Hours* tab (Figure 3-12). Here you can set various business hours for different operations based on different time zones. For instance, if your tech support team is available 24/7, but your head office works only Monday-Friday from 9a.m.-6p.m. PST, you will need to create two different sets of business hours.

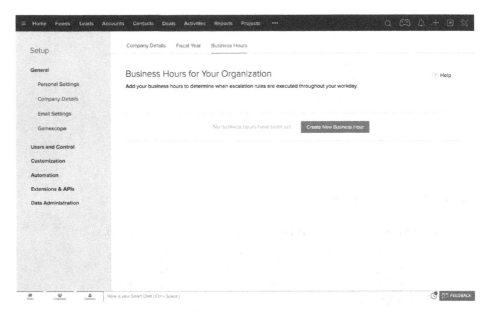

Figure 3-12. *Creating business hours*

12. In the *Business Hours* page, click the *Create New Business Hour* button. *Business Hours Detail* page opens.

13. Enter a meaningful *Name* and the applicable *Time Zone*. Then set the *operational hours* for each applicable day and leave the unoperational hours unchanged (01:00 AM) (Figure 3-13). Finish by clicking *Save*.

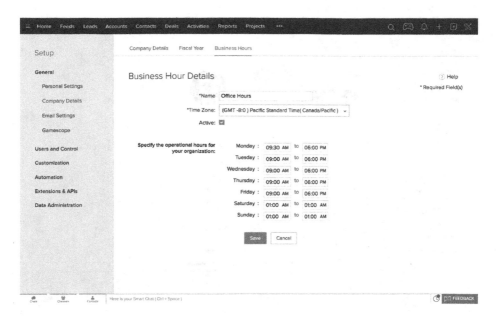

Figure 3-13. *Creating business hours*

User Management

You should create new users for every employee who will use the CRM. Sharing accounts is usually not a good idea due to security and accountability reasons. There are cases when you might want more than one person to access the same account, such as the administrator account, but for salespeople it is always a good idea to assign one account per person.

In CRM, you can define as many users as you like, and the Free edition allows a maximum of 10 users to be created. ten free users are often plenty, because if you have 10 or more employees, you should be investing in one of the paid editions and utilizing more advanced features not available in the Free edition.

Although you may not actually need to add new users to CRM at this stage while you are still learning, it is still a good idea to add one or two of your colleagues to test the features of the CRM together.

Follow these steps to add a new user to CRM:

1. If you are continuing from the previous section, click *Users and Controls* and then *Users* on the sidebar; otherwise, open the *Setup* page and click on *Users* under *USERS AND CONTROL*. A list of users will be displayed (Figure 3-14).

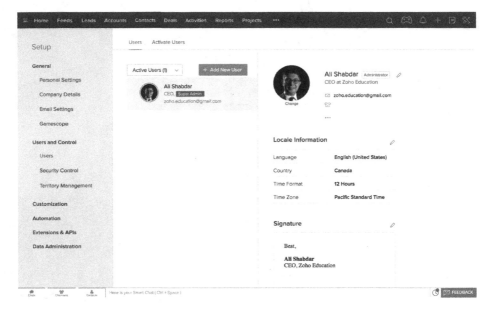

Figure 3-14. *Users settings page*

2. Click the *Add New User* button on top of the list. *Add New User* dialog box will open (Figure 3-15).

Figure 3-15. *Adding a new user*

3. Enter *First Name, Last Name,* and *Email* for the new user.

4. Next, click on the *Roles* button next to the *Role* field. *Roles List* dialog box will open (Figure 3-16).

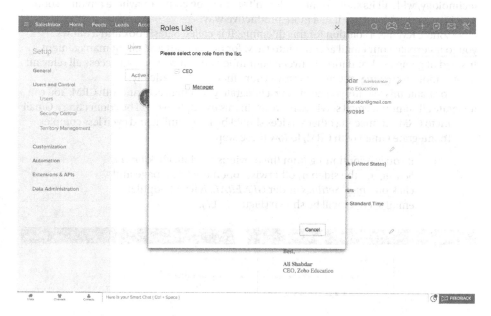

Figure 3-16. Roles List dialog box

5. In *Roles List* box, click on *Manager*. Manager role will be assigned to the new user.

6. Select *Standard* from the *Profile* drop-down list and click *Save* to add the new user.

At this point the new user will be added to the list of users. CRM wil send an invitation email to the new user, which must be accepted before the user can access your CRM.

■ **Note**   Zoho CRM offers versatile user profile and role management to give you complete freedom and flexibility to define reporting rules, as well as to limit users to access the information they don't need, or are not allowed to access. We will learn about these advanced features later in this book.

Email Settings

Despite all the efforts and newer technologies and modern takes on messaging, such as Slack,[3] a majority of business communications still happens via Email. This 50-year-old technology, with all its shortcomings, doesn't seem to be going anywhere anytime soon, so it is smart to at least use it in a more productive way.

Zoho CRM has a solution for this dilemma. It is called SalesInbox and it allows you to incorpate your email account into CRM for better sales and client management. Instead of going back and forth between your inbox and CRM, you can access all relevant information from one place and improve your efficieny dramatically.

To enable this feature, you need to first integrate your email account with CRM. You can integrate all common email services; however, in this example, we will be connecting a Gmail account to CRM. Connecting other services should be fairly similar and even less complex.

To integrate Gmail with CRM, follow these steps:

1. If you are continuing from the previous section, click *Emails Settings* on the sidebar; otherwise, open the *Setup* page and click on *Email Settings* under *GENERAL*. A list of popular email services will be shown (Figure 3-17).

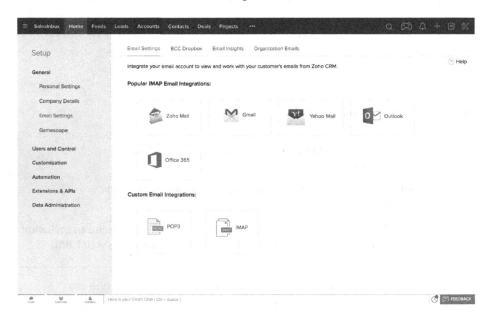

Figure 3-17. *Email settings*

2. Click on Gmail button to continue.

3. In the next page enter your full name, Gmail address, and Gmail password (Figure 3-18). Click *Continue* to proceed.

---

[3]https://slack.com/

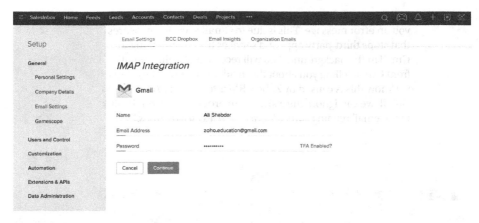

Figure 3-18. *Setting up a Gmail account*

4. The page will expand asking for email sharing permissions (Figure 3-19). Leave the default selection, *Private – Only Me*, as is and click *Continue*.

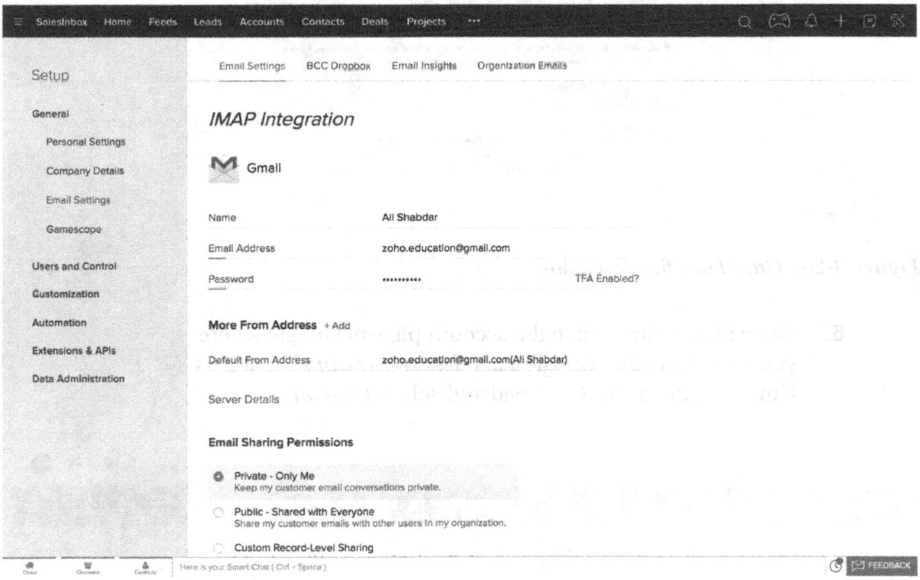

Figure 3-19. *Setting up a Gmail account, step 2*

5. At this stage, the integration wizard may get stuck, even showing you an error message. This is due to Gmail security measures that stops third-party apps and services from connecting to Gmail in the background. You will receive a warning email from Gmail telling you about the incident (Figure 3-20). Since we know this is caused by Zoho CRM attempting to connect to Gmail, we can ignore the warning. To proceed click on the link in the email reading "*allowing access to less secure apps.*"

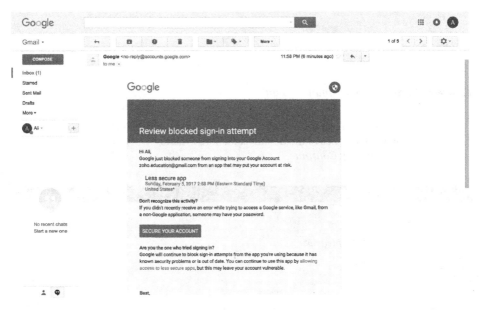

Figure 3-20. *Gmail notification email*

6. You will be redirected to the account page of Google where you can allow what Google calls "*less secure apps*" to access Gmail (Figure 3-21). Go ahead and select *Turn on*.

Figure 3-21. *Enabling less secure apps for Gmail*

7. Then log into Gmail and open *Settings* (Figure 3-22).

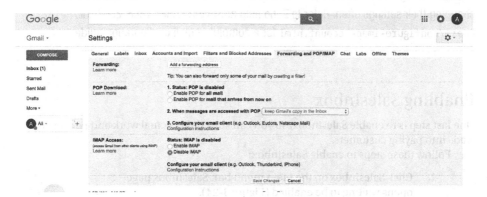

***Figure 3-22.** Enabling IMAP for Gmail*

8. In Gmail *Settings* page, select *Enable IMAP* and click *Save Changes*.

9. Now go back to CRM and click *Proceed* button again. You may need to reenter your Gmail password from before. Upon successful connection a message will indicate that the sync is in progress (Figure 3-23). You can leave this page now. You will receive an email after a successful sync between Gmail and CRM.

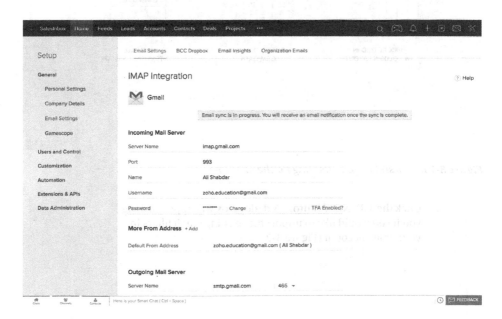

***Figure 3-23.** Finishing email setup*

■ **Note**   Inetgrating emails with CRM could prove tricky, especially with email services changing their settings often. Refer to Zoho help at `https://www.zoho.com/crm/help/email/configure-imap-account.html` for a complete email configuration guide.

Enabling SalesInbox

One last step is to enable SalesInbox, so you can start doing actual work and converting leads into paying customers.

Follow these steps to enable SalesInbox:

1.   Click SalesInbox on the main menu bar. SalesInbox page opens waiting to be enabled (Figure 3-24).

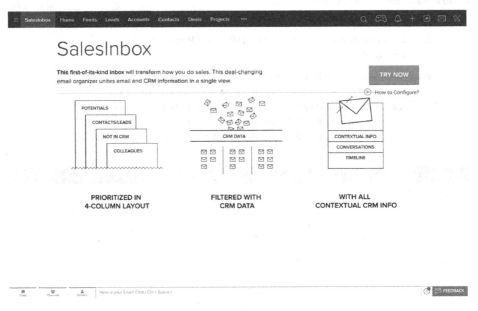

Figure 3-24. *SalesInbox page loading for the first time*

2.   Click the TRY NOW button. A dialog box will appear asking you if you would like to import the existing email filters in your email account (Figure 3-25).

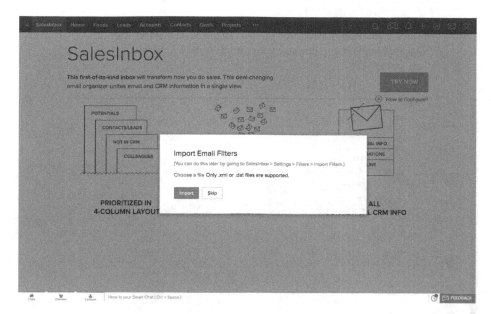

Figure 3-25. *Importing email filters*

3. Click *Skip* for now. You can import filters (if you have any) later from the SalesInbox settings page. A moment later the SalesInbox page will refresh, showing your emails in a familiar inbox interface, only with more features for CRM (Figure 3-26).

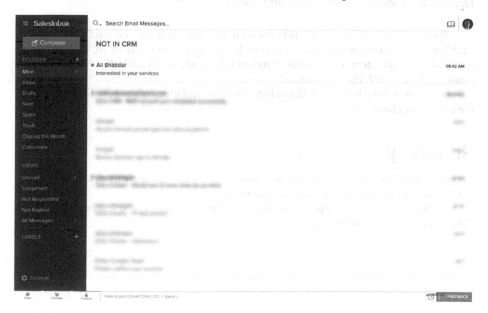

Figure 3-26. *SalesInbox page populated with emails*

4. Click on of the emails to see more details about a specific email. All essential features, such as Reply and Forward, are available for you to manage your emails from within CRM (Figure 3-27).

Figure 3-27. *Familiar interface, familiar features*

There are, however, two curious buttons on the top right of the screen: *LEAD* and *CONTACT*. These buttons let you add the sender of the email directly to the CRM process. After that point all interactions between you and the lead (or contact) will be logged and managed in the CRM. Pretty awesome!

Our work is done here. We will use these buttons and other features of SalesInbox in the upcoming chapters.

Summary

In this chapter, you created your very first Zoho CRM and made some essential confirgurations to make it ready for the next steps.

In the next chapter, we will start using SalesInbox, modules and other features of CRM to manage our sales funnel.

CHAPTER 4

■ ■ ■

Running Your Business on Zoho CRM

It is hard to argue that the core objective of every serious business is to generate profit. Therefore, it is paramount to meticulously manage the entire sales process, from inception to post sales.

If you closely look at your business processes you will see, not surprisingly, that almost every process is, directly or indirectly, contributing to increase sales. Otherwise you should seriously review that process.

In this chapter, we will see how Zoho CRM manages the sales force to make your life easier and help you increase sales. This is one of the most important chapters in the book. Make sure you understand the concepts and practice as much as it takes.

Managing the Sales Pipeline

Zoho CRM is fairly similar to other powerful CRM systems out there in terms of features and capabilities of managing your sales processes. If you come from another CRM system, you will notice some differences in lingo and other areas; however, the essence of CRM practice is more or less the same in all of these systems.

At the core of Zoho CRM lie powerful sales force automation modules and tools, allowing you to fully manage your pipeline (or, funnel), that is, all the stages from when leads are collected until a deal is closed and beyond.

You should design the stages of your pipeline according to your sales processes; however, it is safe to say that there are four common stages to consider for a typical sales pipeline:

- Lead Generation
- Lead Qualification
- Opportunities (or Deals)
- Sales

© Ali Shabdar 2017
A. Shabdar, *Mastering Zoho CRM*, DOI 10.1007/978-1-4842-2904-0_4

Figure 4-1 shows a typical pipeline based on the four stages previously mentioned.

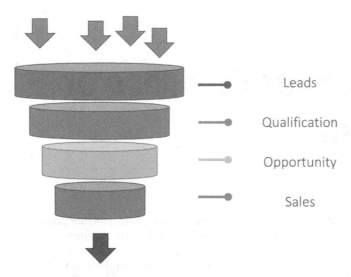

Figure 4-1. *A typical sales pipeline*

One key importance of the funnel (or pipeline) is that as a business owner, or decision maker, you can have a bird's eye view of your business at any given moment and see who is where in the funnel and how close a deal is to closing. Maintaining and managing an accurate funnel helps you monitor the performance of your business and strategize accordingly, with clarity and agility.

Leads

Leads are people or companies whom fall in your target market and might turn into prospects interested in your products or services. Every business card you collect, every email address that gets registered on your website, or any one result of executive searches on LinkedIn are considered leads.

All leads should be captured in the CRM from the early stage, one by one, or in bulk and then be taken through the sales funnel until they turn into sales (or not).

Lead Qualification

The second stage in the funnel is Qualification. In this stage, you (or the person to whom specific leads are assigned) validates leads by contacting them, following up, and evaluating their interest level, decision-making power, and buying appetite.

You should be capturing every action done on the lead in the CRM. This information will help you qualify leads and push them to the next stage, or simply disqualify them and move on to the next lead.

Opportunities

After a lead is qualified, it needs to get "converted." Conversion turns a qualified lead into a contact, an account, and an opportunity (or, potential) for a deal. In the "conversion" process, Zoho CRM generates the corresponding Contact, Account, and Opportunity in the click of a button.

A lot needs to happen between a lead becoming an opportunity and the actual sales happening. Further follow-ups are often needed, followed by sending quotes, sales orders, invoices, and hopefully a closed deal at the end.

These steps are documented in a logical and connected way in the CRM, centralizing important data and connecting the dots more effectively while keeping valuable information safe for future use.

Getting Started with Sales Force Automation

When you first open Zoho CRM (by logging onto `http://creator.zoho.com`), you are welcomed by the *Getting Started* page (Figure 4-2) inviting you to perform a number of common tasks. For now, you can ignore this page.

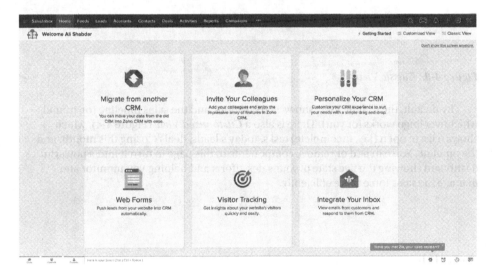

Figure 4-2. *Getting Started page*

■ **Warning**   Although Zoho CRM offers powerful tools out-of-the-box for you to get started almost immediately and use it in day-to-day business, it is imperative to understand all the relevant aspects of your business processes and customize CRM accordingly. These customizations could be as simple as renaming a module name, or as sophisticated as creating custom modules and adding complex workflows. We will learn how to make Zoho CRM the rock solid tool your business needs as we go forward.

To start, click on the *Classic View* link on the top right of the *Getting Started* page to switch the view.

The Classic View shows the bird's eye view of your business. Of course, there is not much to see here when you first start (Figure 4-3): however, after populating CRM you will start seeing valuable information in real time.

Figure 4-3. *Classic View*

By default, the Classic View shows tasks, events, and the sales pipeline (or, funnel, whichever lingo works for you). There is also a *Customized View* (Figure 4-4), which shows a list of open (i.e., incomplete) tasks, today's leads, deals closing this month, and the pipeline. You can add or remove components to this page to turn it into a powerful dashboard showing the live state of your sales efforts and helping you monitor and manage the sales force more efficiently.

Figure 4-4. *Customized View*

Managing Leads

As mentioned in a previous section, lead management is an inseparable part of the CRM process in general and obviously Zoho CRM itself. *Leads* module is one of the essential modules in Zoho CRM and is closely connected with other modules, such as *Deals*.

Any organization that does some sort of sales of goods and services must take managing leads seriously. No matter the quantity and quality of the leads generated, if they are not managed properly, chances are that the business is losing valuable opportunities that can turn into profitable deals in the short or the long run.

Adding a New Lead

Let's start exploring the essential lead management features of Zoho CRM by creating a single lead manually:

1. Click on the + (plus sign) on the right-hand side of the main menu bar and then select *Lead* from the drop-down menu (Figure 4-5). Alternatively, you can open the Leads page (from the top menu bar) and click the *New Lead* button.

Figure 4-5. *Creating a new lead*

2. In the *Create Lead* page (Figure 4-6), put in as much information as you have about a lead, especially *Company* and *Lead Name*, as they are both mandatory fields for a lead.

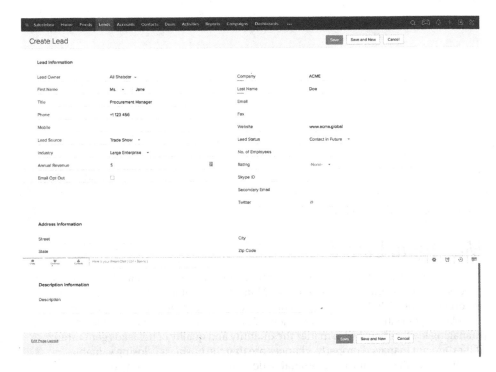

Figure 4-6. *Populating the lead form*

3. Once you are done with entering all the available information for the lead, click on the *Save* button in the bottom of the form. The new lead gets created and displayed in the lead details page (Figure 4-7).

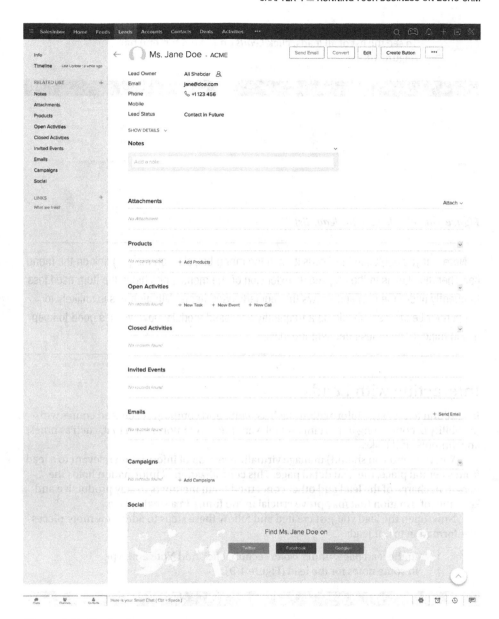

Figure 4-7. *The lead page*

4. You can repeat these steps and add as many leads as you need. To see the list of all leads, click *Leads* on the main menu bar (Figure 4-8).

Figure 4-8. *First lead in the leads list*

■ **Note** If you don't see the *Leads* item in the menu bar, click on the (…) link on the menu bar. Then find Leads in the drop-down extension of the menu. Zoho hides the item used less frequently under the (…) and shows the regularly used items. Although this is unlikely to happen for Leads, as it should be a frequently accessed module; however, it's good to keep this in mind for other less frequent modules.

Interacting with Leads

In addition to the basic information, such as name and company, each lead comes with the ability of connecting important and relevant pieces of information to it, such as notes, attachments, and tasks.

You can (and you should) manage virtually every bit of information relevant to a lead from a central place, the lead detail page. This centralization of information helps the person in charge of the lead and other concerned team members to stay productive and keep the information that may prove crucial in the future in a single place.

Now, open the lead you just created and follow these steps to add a few more pieces of information to our lead:

1. In the lead page, under *Notes* section, click Add Note and type in some notes for the lead (Figure 4-9).

Figure 4-9. *Adding notes for a lead*

2. Under the *Attachment* section, click Attach. A drop-down menu opens, providing you with different ways of attaching a document to this lead, including uploading from your computer, or from cloud storage services, such as Zoho Docs and Google Drive (Figure 4-10). Choose one of the scenarios and attach one or more files to the lead.

Figure 4-10. *Attaching files to a lead*

3. Under *Open Activities*, there are three types of activities to choose from: *Task, Event,* and *Call.* You can add a list of to dos, log of phone calls, and events (e.g., future meetings) with the specific lead in here. Click *New Task* to continue.

4. In the *Create Task* form, type in the mandatory *Subject* of the task and other optional fields (Figure 4-11). You can set up a due date and a reminder for the task. Zoho CRM will send you notifications to remind you about an approaching task. Click Save when you are done.

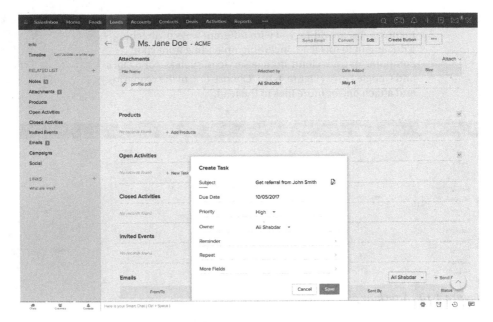

Figure 4-11. *Adding tasks for a lead*

5. When you complete an open activity and change its status
    to Complete, it automatically moves under *Closed Activities*
    (Figure 4-12). Open the task you created in the previous step
    and set it to *Complete*. It will automatically move from *Open
    Activities* to *Closed Activities*.

Figure 4-12. *Closed Activites for a lead*

6. Last, but not least, you can send emails to a lead from within the lead page. This is great, because it helps you keep a complete log of your communications with a specific lead in one place along with everything else about the lead. Under *Emails* click *Send Email*. In the Send Email dialog box (Figure 4-13), type in your message. Click *Send* after you are happy with the content of your message and it will be sent to your lead immediately.

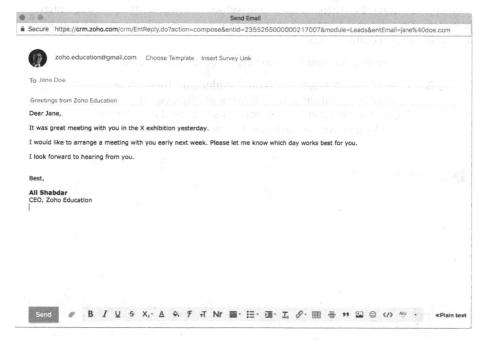

Figure 4-13. Sending email to a lead

Feel free to add more items for the lead and see how each section works.

Importing Multiple Leads

Adding leads one by one is a straightforward task in Zoho CRM. There is also the Zoho CRM mobile app for the people on the go, so you can add new leads on your way back from a successful meeting instead of spending time on Instagram.

But how about when you need to add multiple leads quickly and efficiently? For instance, if a large list of leads is generated from an email campaign, or you have a helpful admin person to digitize a million business cards you accumulated in a recent exhibition you attended?

Thankfully, Zoho CRM has a feature that allows you to import leads in bulk sans the joy of keying them in one by one. This is particularly easy if you have the list of leads in an Excel or CSV (Comma Separated Values) file. The data in such a list must be properly organized and all mandatory fields (Lead Name and Company are mandatory by default) are populated for each row.

Let's learn how this is done in Zoho CRM. If you have your leads already stored nicely and cleanly in an Excel or CSV file, you can ignore the first three steps of the following instruction set and go directly to step 4.

Otherwise, for the purpose of this exercise, we need to first create a dummy list and then import it into CRM. There is a lifesaving website called *generatedata.com*, which helps you create dummy data tables populated with random information. We use this site to create our list of dummy leads:

1. In your web browser, log onto http://generatedata.com.

2. Under *Generate* tab, enter "*Leads*" as filename, then create data columns starting with *First Name* as displayed in Figure 4-14. You can add new rows to add more data columns by clicking *Row(s)* button below the list.

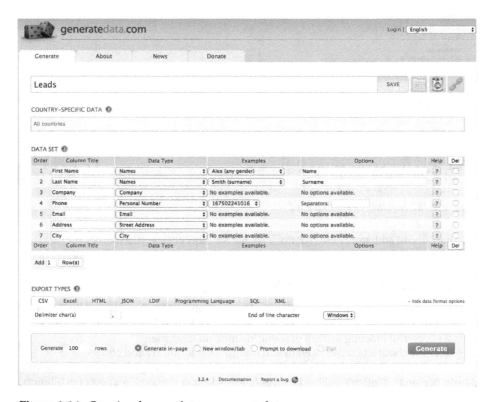

Figure 4-14. *Creating dummy data on generatedata.com*

3. When you are finished with adding all the data columns, make sure the *CSV* tab is selected under *Export Types*, then enter a single comma (,) for *Delimiter char(s)*.

4. Leave other fields as they are and click the *Generate* button on the bottom of the page. The list will be generated within seconds and automatically downloads to your computer. Depending on your operating system and browser settings, you may get a message box asking you to confirm the download.

5. Open the downloaded CSV file. The data should look like Figure 4-15. Quite good for random information!

	A	B	C	D	E	F	G
1	First Name	Last Name	Company	Phone	Email	Address	City
2	Kathleen	Gentry	Parturient Montes Associates	1643020298099	erat@magnaaneque.ca	4554 Ac Road	Casoli
3	Victoria	Mckee	Aenean Eget Consulting	1610051461199	cursus@eudui.net	P.O. Box 612, 451 Sit Road	GrivegnÅ½e
4	Clarke	Barrett	Erat Sed Industries	1642070316799	non@tinciduntnibh.ca	Ap #928-8921 Luctus Street	Birmingham
5	Jackson	Frank	Tortor At PC	1679070876899	Aliquam.nisl.Nulla@IpsumSuspendissenon.edu	Ap #784-2880 Morbi Street	Koolgem
6	Oscar	Booth	Nec Mollis Incorporated	1697042544499	enim@Crasdictumultricies.edu	795-7798 Cras Avenue	Oetingen
7	Hanna	Rogers	At LLC	1683051049699	sodales.nisl.magna@arcuet.com	Ap #754-7347 Cum Av.	Piracicaba
8	Pandora	Francis	Lacinia At Iaculis Foundation	1630061370299	iaculis@natoque.ca	Ap #720-2650 Eget Avenue	Rankweil
9	Aiko	Grimes	Vel Convallis PC	1627080747199	vitae.sodales.at@quis.edu	691-2527 Sem Rd.	Montaldo Bormida
10	Edward	Charles	Diam At Pretium Industries	1635051649599	bibendum.fermentum@Loremipsumdolor.ca	Ap #718-8452 Nunc St.	Stirling
11	Wade	Hunter	In Dolor LLC	1653091460199	ligula@orci.edu	P.O. Box 913, 7969 Arcu St.	Bruderheim
12	Meghan	Carson	Lectus Limited	1699021653199	Nam.porttitor@risusodio.com	P.O. Box 761, 7433 Faucibus Rd.	Courcelles
13	Germane	Newton	Eget Venenatis A Foundation	1645112010199	facilisis.non.bibendum@Cumsociisnatoque.co.uk	P.O. Box 987, 7358 Cursus, Rd.	Windsor
14	Risa	Mckee	Eros Company	1676081275599	mus@ut.ca	776-3701 Orci, Av.	Ergani

Figure 4-15. *Snapshot of the dummy data*

6. Now switch back to Zoho CRM, open the Leads page, and click on the *Import* button on the top right of the leads list. The *Import Leads* wizard will open (Figure 4-16).

Figure 4-16. *Import Leads wizard*

7. In the Import Leads page, select Import My Leads, which will set the lead owner to your name.

8. Click *Choose File* button to select the leads CSV file you downloaded (or you had from before).

9. Select *Overwrite* for *Duplicate Record,* and set *Find duplicates using* to *Email.*

■ **Note** This setting will tell CRM to consider two (or more) leads the same if they have the same email address and then overwrite the older lead (if already existing in the CRM) with the new one that is just being imported. This doesn't mean that the older lead will be completely replaced by the new one, rather only the fields that exist on both existing and the importing leads will take the value of the importing lead. For this particular example, where we are working with dummy data, we don't worry about existing information, but in an operational system where valuable lead information already exists, a simple overwrite could delete existing information partially or completely. So, depending on the scenario choose *Clone* or *Skip* for duplicate leads.

---

10. Click *Next* to continue. The import wizard will upload the CSV file and load the columns it found in the file for you to map to the matching fields in the CRM *Leads* module (Figure 4-17).

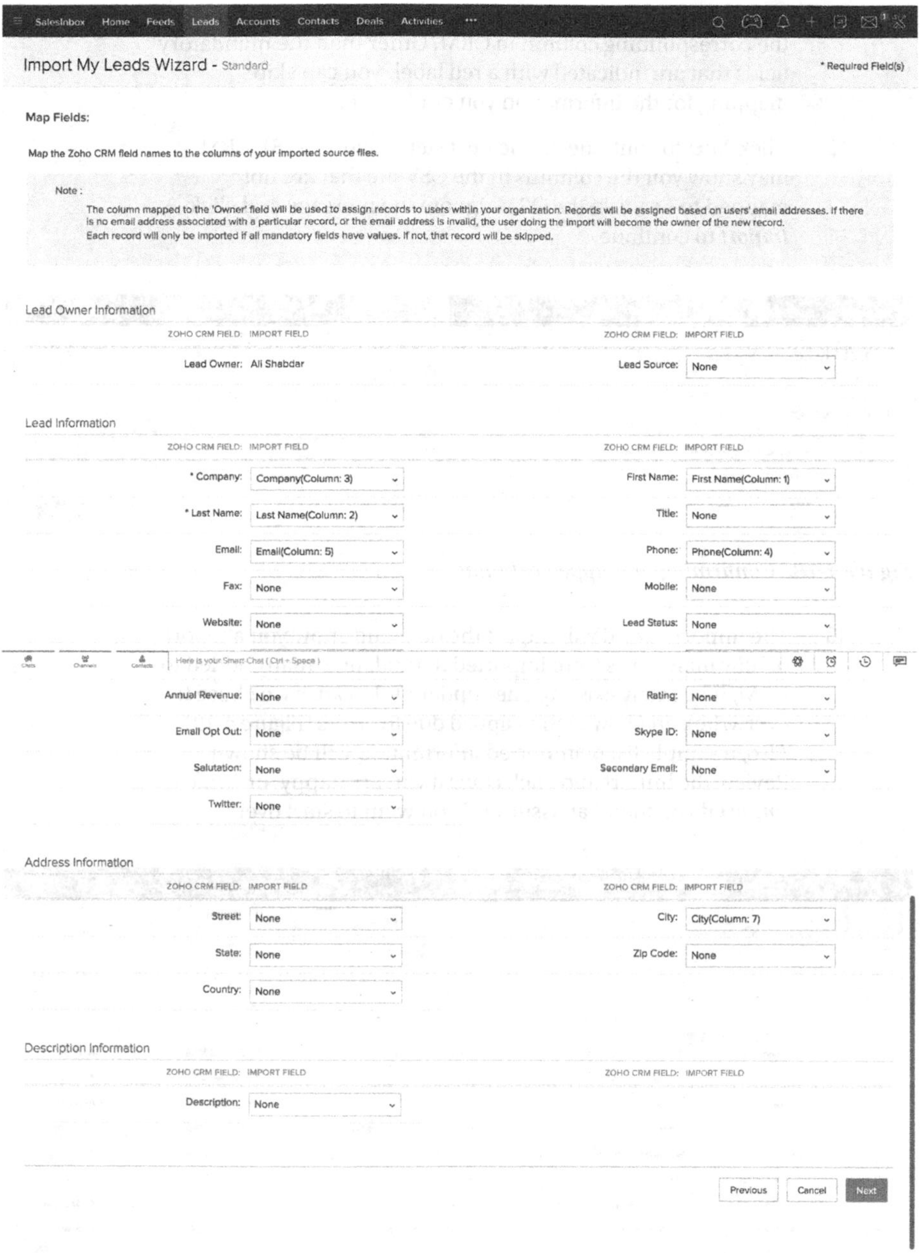

Figure 4-17. Mapping fields

11. Review the fields and make sure each column is mapped to the corresponding column in CRM. Other than the mandatory fields that are indicated with a red label, you can skip mapping for the information you don't have.

12. Click *Next* to continue. In the next step (Figure 4-18), CRM may show you the columns in the CSV file that are not mapped to Leads in the CRM. Ignore the message and click *Import* to continue.

Figure 4-18. *Confirming unmapped columns*

13. The import wizard will import the data and show you a report of how many rows were imported in total, how many added to CRM, how many existing ones updated (because we chose to overwrite), and how many skipped due to errors (Figure 4-19). Also, a sample list of imported information will be shown. Review the import and click *Done* if you are happy, or *Undo Import* if you found an issue and you want to start over.

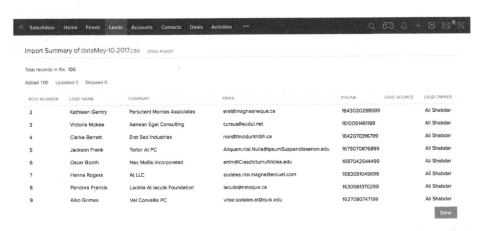

Figure 4-19. *Bulk leads import complete*

Great. The import is done and you can start working with them (Figure 4-20). Feel free to navigate through leads, change values, and delete some of them to familiarize yourself more with the Leads module.

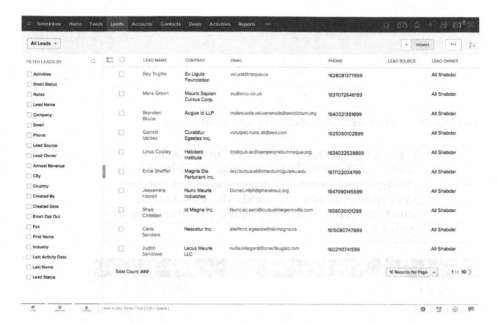

Figure 4-20. *List of all leads in the CRM*

Bulk Operations

From the previous section, you can see that in our newly imported list, *Lead Source* is missing, because it was not in the CSV file and the import wizard left the value empty for all imported records.

Since lead source is an important piece of information, we want to populate this value for the leads. One way is to open each lead and set the *Lead Source*, but that is too much work, especially if lead source for all of these leads is the same (a trade show, or online campaign). Such scenarios happen often and you need bulk operations to perform repeated data manipulation faster and stay productive.

Mass Updating Leads

Fortunately, Zoho CRM offer mass updating features for leads and other modules, so we can go about changing the lead source of all newly important leads in one go following these steps:

1. In the Leads page, click on the ... button on the top right of the page and select *Mass Update* in the drop-down menu (Figure 4-21).

Figure 4-21. Starting the mass update process for leads

2. In the next page (Figure 4-22), under Criteria Component select *Lead Owner* for the first criterion, then select *is* and then type in your name. This means that the mass update will be performed only on the leads whose owner is the current user, preserving other people's leads from being mass updated.

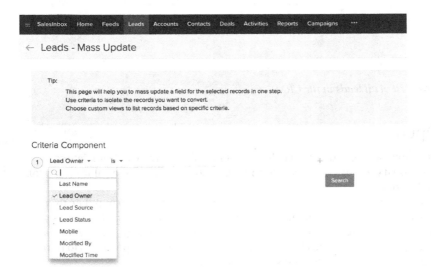

Figure 4-22. Choosing the Lead Owner as a search criterion.

3. Click the green (+) button next to criterion #1 to add another criterion. Then select *Lead Status*, and *is empty* (Figure 4-23). This ensures a mass update happens only on your leads whose Lead Status is not set yet, sparing the ones with existing lead status.

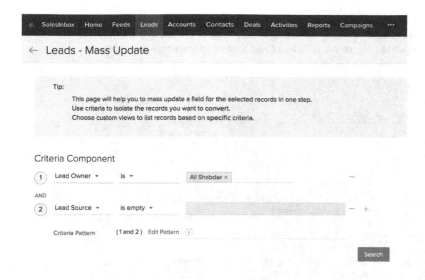

Figure 4-23. *Choosing only the leads with no Lead Source*

4. Click Search to see a list of leads that match the above criteria (Figure 4-24).

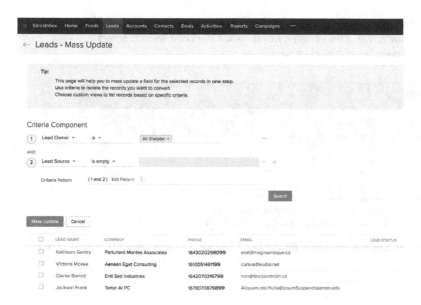

Figure 4-24. *List of leads found based on the search criteria ready for mass update*

5. Click *Mass Update* button on the top-left side of the list. A dialog box will open asking which field you want to mass update (Figure 4-25). Select *Lead Source* in the drop-down list.

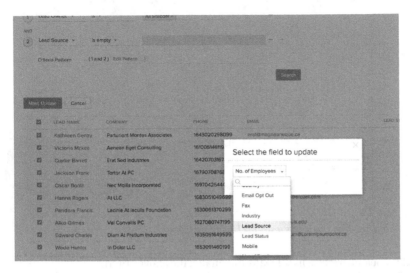

Figure 4-25. *Choosing Lead Source to be updated for all selected leads*

6. In the next screen (Figure 4-26), a drop-down list will be shown with a list of different values for the Lead Source. Select "*Trade Show*" and click *Save*.

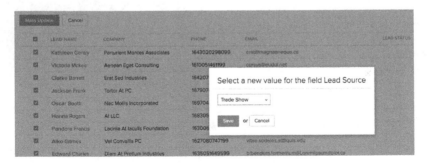

Figure 4-26. *Setting the new value for the Lead Source field to be applied to all selected leads*

After clicking save, as you can see in Figure 4-27, all leads matching the criteria set above will have their Lead Status set to "Trade Show."

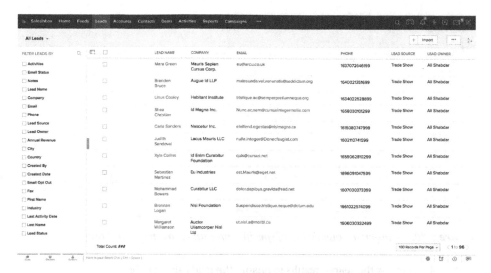

Figure 4-27. *Mass update took effect for all the leads selected previously.*

Mass Transferring Leads

In Zoho CRM, each lead has an owner who is a registered Zoho CRM user. By default the lead owner of a new lead (or leads) is the user who created the lead. This, of course, can change by editing a lead and transferring the lead ownership to someone else; however, there are times that you need to transfer multiple leads to another user.

Suppose for the leads you imported previously, you need to distribute them among the sales team, so they can start contacting them and hopefully turn them into sales. A number of factors may be considered when distributing leads, such as geographical territory, type of lead, etc. In the following example, we will transfer a number of leads to a team member using the simple logic of transferring only the leads whose company names starts with an "a." Not exactly a scientific method of leads distribution, but it serves the purpose here.

1. In the Leads page, click on the ... button on the top right of the page and select *Mass Transfer* from the drop-down list.

2. In the *Leads Mass Transfer* page, put in your user name in *Transfer From* and the user name of the new lead owner in *Transfer To*.

3. Under *Specify Criteria*, select *Company* and starts with, then enter "*a*" in the value text box and click *Search* (Figure 4-28).

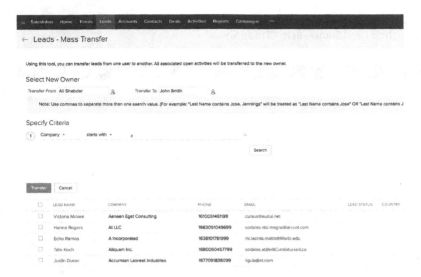

Figure 4-28. *Transferring ownership of specific companies to a new CRM user*

4. Review the search results to ensure the leads about to be transferred are correct. Then click Transfer to proceed. The leads will transfer to the new owner (Figure 4-29).

Figure 4-29. *Some leads have new owners now.*

Finding Leads

Soon you will have tens and hundreds of leads in the CRM waiting for your champion salespeople to turn into lucrative sales and loyal customers. More leads means you can no longer rely on the list of leads to find who you are looking for. A good CRM system must offer advanced and fast search tools and Zoho CRM is no exception.

Searching for Leads

In Zoho CRM, the quickest way of finding leads (and other information) is to use the global search. The global search is accessible throughout CRM by clicking on the magnifier button on the top menu bar (Figure 4-30). Simply type in the name of a lead, company, source, or basically anything you can remember about the information you are looking for.

Figure 4-30. *Searching for a term in the entire CRM*

By default, any piece of information that contains the search term (*"acme,"* in this example) in any of its data fields will be pulled from across the CRM and listed in the search results. You can see in Figure 4-31 that the search results shows account, contacts, deals, and tasks. The result will vary for you as you have different information stored in your CRM account.

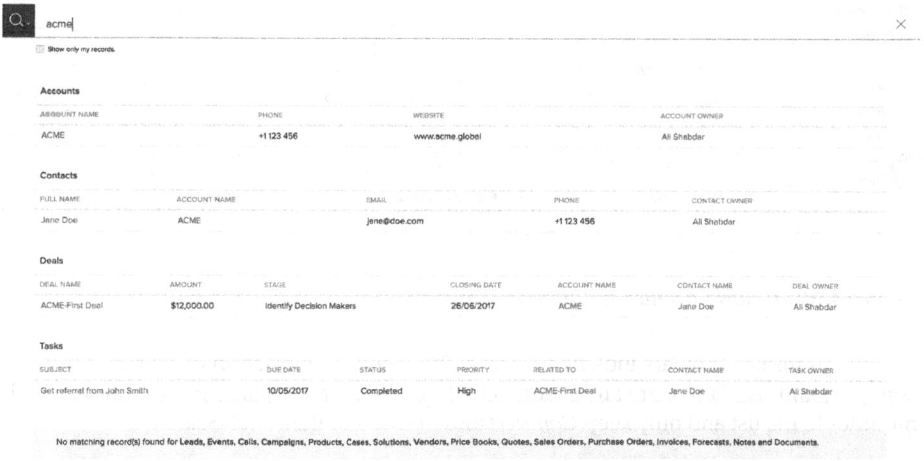

Figure 4-31. *Global search results*

On the results page, you can click on any of the results found and access the corresponding information. For instance, clicking on a task will open the detail's respective task.

Notice at the bottom of the results page, there is a gray info-bar listing the modules (e.g. Leads, Events, etc.) in which the search didn't find any results. This means there were no leads in my account (i.e., current user) that contains *"acme"* in any shape or form.

Narrowing Down the Search Scope

Searching the CRM globally is quite handy and often finds the information you are looking for; however, these results can get crowded depending on the size of the information kept in the CRM and also how generic the search term is.

One good way of quickly narrowing down the scope of your search is to choose which CRM module the global search should look into. To do so, in the search results page, click the magnifier icon on the top left of the screen and choose the target modules (Figure 4-32).

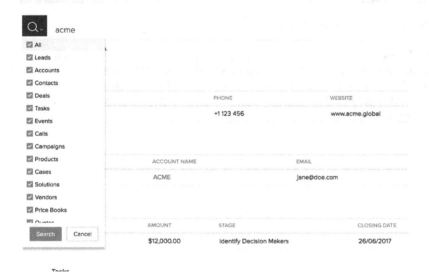

Figure 4-32. *Choosing which modules to search in*

For example, if you are looking to extract the contact information of everyone in a company and see if there are any events scheduled for that company, you can deselect all modules in the list and only keep *Contacts* and *Events* and then click *Search*.

Filtering Through Leads

As mentioned previously the global is powerful and easy to use, but it is designed for quick on-off searches. If you tend to look for specific information in a module (including Leads) regularly, there is a better way to find the right information: Filters.

As the name suggests, filters let you filter the long list of leads and see only what you are looking for more quickly and more efficiently. The big advantage of filters is that they can be saved for later use, without the need for entering the search term every time.

To see them in action, let's apply a filter to the list of leads:

1. In the Leads page, select *Lead Owner* in the list of fields on the left side of the screen and then select *is* and type in a user name (Figure 4-33). The list of leads immediately changes, showing only the leads that match the filter.

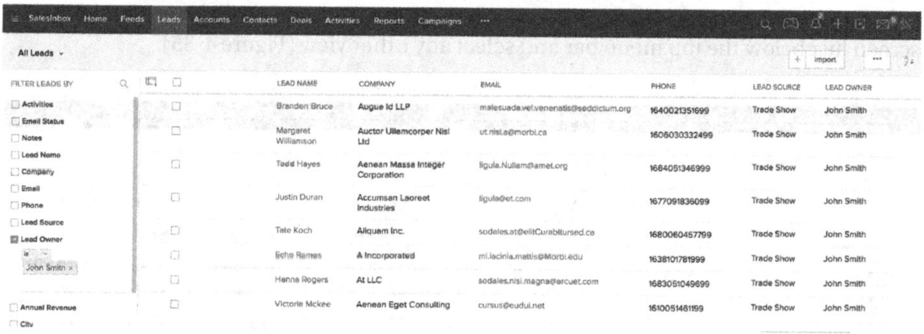

***Figure 4-33.** Filtering leads by Lead Owner*

2. To use this filter again in the future, click *Save Filter* button on the bottom left of the screen and enter a suitable filter name (Figure 4-34). Click *Save Filter* to proceed.

***Figure 4-34.** Saving the filter for later use*

The new filter will be listed under filters and is ready to use in the click of a button.

Views

As you have seen a number of times in this chapter before, when you open the *Leads* module, by default a list of leads is shown in the leads page.

These lists are called *Views* and are one of the powerful features of Zoho CRM. As the name suggests, View gives different ways of viewing your information. One of the fundamental characteristics of good software is that users enter information once (e.g., add new leads) and output this information in different ways. The difference in output of information is often about formatting, order, data set, and output medium.

For instance, one view will show all the leads in the system, while another will only show the current user's leads entered today. Also a view can output its data on the screen, to a CSV file, or a PDF document to be sent by email to a third party.

Let's start our tour of the Views by having a look at two of the most common existing views in Zoho CRM.

The first one is All Views, which is accessible by simply opening the Leads module. To open other views, you need to click on the view selector button on the top left of the screen just below the top menu bar and select any other view (Figure 4-35).

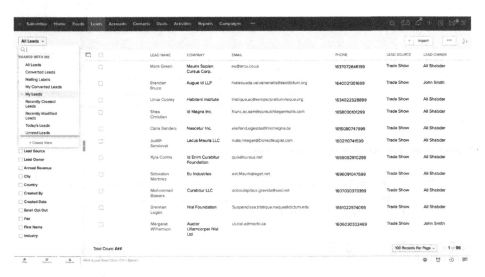

Figure 4-35. *Choosing My Leads view*

Figure 4-36 show *My Leads* view, which shows the list of leads belonging to the current user.

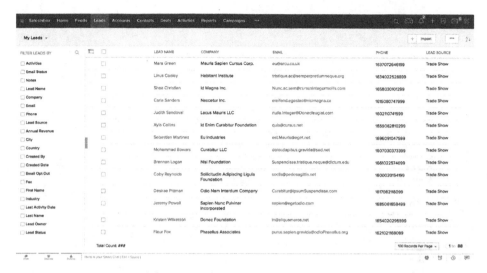

Figure 4-36. *My Leads view*

You can see that in the view, the Lead Owner column is not shown simply because we already know who the lead owner is. Another characteristic of good software is to show only the relevant and necessary information and avoid information clutter as much as possible. You will see in the upcoming sections that you can customize and create views. Keeping this small but important point in mind helps you create useful views for your users.

Customizing Views

There is a good collection of preexisting views in Zoho CRM; however, every business has different needs and sooner or later you will need views of your own. The quickest way to have your own views is to customize the existing ones.

To modify *My Leads*, which is an existing view, follow these steps:

1. Open the *My Leads* view.

2. Click the ... button on the top right of the view and select *Edit View*. The view editor will open for My Leads view (Figure 4-37).

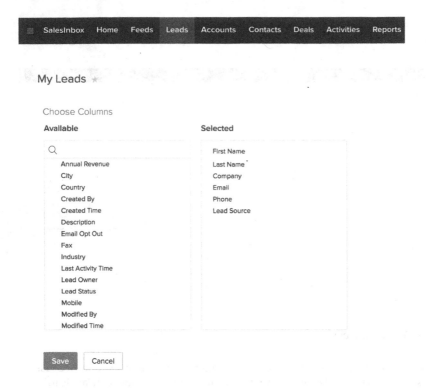

Figure 4-37. *Editing My Leads view*

3. Under *Choose Columns* section, select *Lead Status* from *Available* fields to add it to *Selected* fields (Figure 4-38).

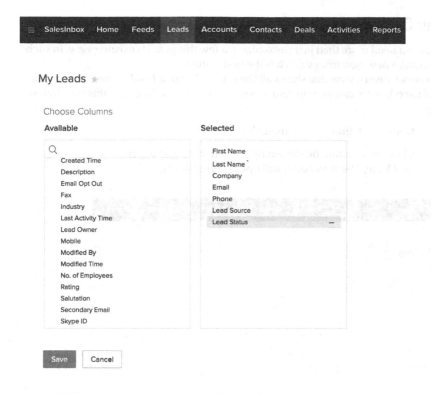

Figure 4-38. *Adding a new column to My Leads view*

4. Click *Save* to apply the changes. *Lead Status* column is now added to the *My Leads* view (Figure 4-39).

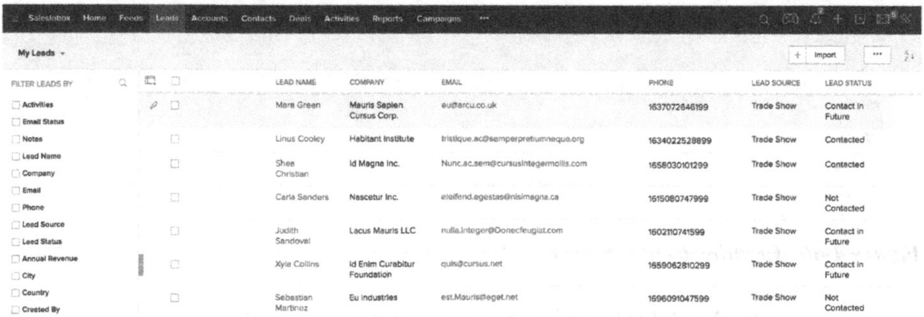

Figure 4-39. *Edited My Leads view in action*

Creating Custom Views

Sometimes you need more than just customizing a few things in an existing view. In such a case, creating a new view from scratch is the best option.

Suppose we need a view that shows all the leads without a *Lead Status* in the system (i.e., for all users), so we can identify and assign status to them. To create this view follow these steps:

1. Open *Leads* from the top menu bar.

2. Click the ... button on the top right of the view and select *Add View*. The view editor will open (Figure 4-40).

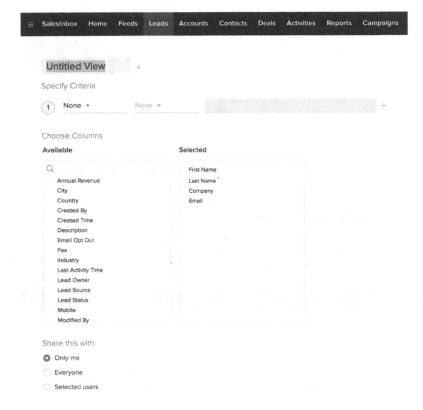

Figure 4-40. *Creating a custom view*

3. Enter "*No-status Leads*" in view name textbox where it currently reads *Untitled View* (Figure 4-41).

4. Under *Specify Criteria*, select *Lead Source* and *is empty*.

No-status Leads ☆

Specify Criteria

① Lead Status ▾   is empty ▾   +

Choose Columns

Available   **Selected**

🔍   First Name

Email Opt Out   Last Name *

. Fax   Company

Industry   Email

Last Activity Time   Lead Source

Lead Owner

Lead Status

Mobile

Modified By

Modified Time

No. of Employees

Phone

Rating

Salutation

Secondary Email

Skype ID

Share this with:

🔘 Only me

◯ Everyone

◯ Selected users

[Save]   Cancel

Figure 4-41. *Setting view properties*

> 5. Under *Choose Columns*, select and add *First Name, Last Name, Company, Email,* and *Leads Source* from the *Available* list to the *Selected* list.
>
> 6. Under Share this with, select Only me to make this view available only to you (the current user).
>
> 7. Click *Save* to create the new view. The view will be added to the list of existing views and open for use (Figure 4-42).

Figure 4-42. *The new custom view in action*

EXERCISE

As a supervisor, you need a view to show you if there are leads entered in the CRM with no action taken on them for more than 7 days, and then act accordingly.

Create a new view that shows open leads created before 7 days ago, with no action taken on them, that is, no status change, visible only to you, the admin user. Show lead name, email address, owner, source, and status.

Converting Leads

If you remember from the beginning of this chapter, we talked about various stages of the sales funnel. After Lead generation and qualification comes opportunity creation, which is the result of successfully converting qualified leads.

In Zoho CRM, once you deem a lead qualified, you can "convert" it manually. This will create up to three new objects in the CRM: a new contact, an account, and a deal (opportunity).

To convert a lead, follow these steps:

1. Open a lead you want to convert and in the lead detail page (Figure 4-43), click on the green *Convert* button.

Figure 4-43. *Lead details page*

2. In the *Convert Lead* page (Figure 4-44), review the first two rows of information indicating that a new account and a new contact are going to be created in the process of conversion.

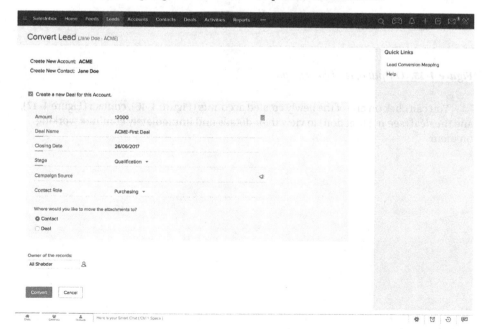

Figure 4-44. *Converting a lead*

3. Check (select) *Create a new Deal for this Account* and enter the deal information as you see in Figure 4-44. Notice the important fields that indicate the projected amount of this deal (opportunity), projected closing date, and the current stage of the deal.

4. Select *Contact* or *Deal* to move the existing attachments in the lead (if any) to the new contact or the deal.

5. Set the *Owner of the records*, that is, the user who will be owning the account, contact, and the deal in the CRM.

6. Click *Convert* to convert the lead and create corresponding records. A confirmation screen will show the output of the conversion (Figure 4-45).

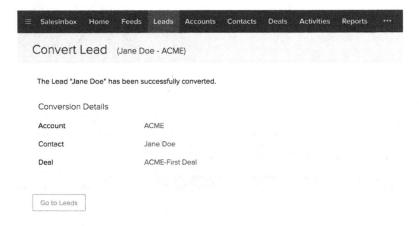

Figure 4-45. *Output of lead conversion*

You can click on any of the newly created accounts (Figure 4-46), contact (Figure 4-47), and the deal (see next section) to view their details and immediately continue working on them.

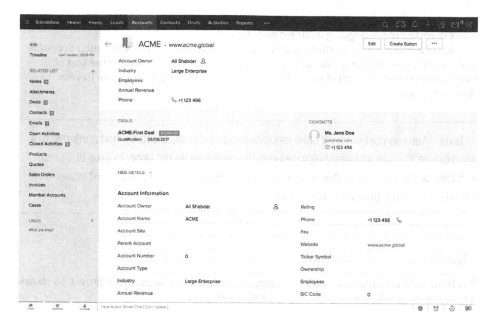

Figure 4-46. *The Account created during lead conversion*

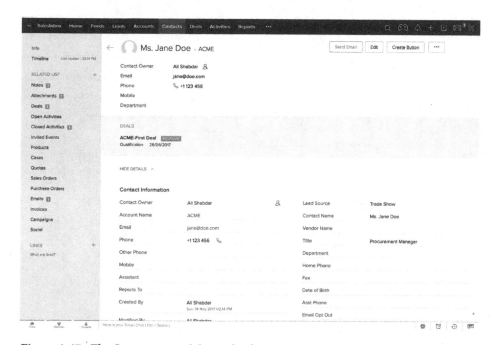

Figure 4-47. *The Contact created during lead conversion*

Notice how both the account and the contact have a section for deals giving you a quick overview of the ongoing deals for each record.

Similar to leads, you can fully manage (edit, export, print, send email, etc.) accounts and contacts from within the detail page. Spend a few minutes reviewing the sort of information stored for each of these records and see how you can use them in your day-to-day business.

■ **Note**   You can customize all Zoho modules, such as leads, accounts, and contacts, to a good extent. You can add new fields; remove the ones that do not apply to your business; and change the behavior of the existing one, for example, make a specific field mandatory. We will learn about this in a later chapter.

Deals

Deals hold the live summary of what is happening with an opportunity. Figure 4-48 shows all the details of a deal we created in the previous section.

Figure 4-48. *The Deal created during lead conversion*

Vital information, such as contact information, current stage of the deal in the pipeline, the history of stage change, notes, tasks, and other related information are all listed here in one place.

There are also other pieces of information that you can add to the deal as you go forward. Among other things, you can manage the list of competitors who may impact the deal, products being sold in this deal, sales order sent to the potential client, and the email correspondence. Once a lead is converted, this page will be the command center for the user in charge of the deal.

Keeping the Stage Up to Date

As you go forward with the deal in real life, the stage in which the deal is in the CRM should change too. This is particularly important to keep the sales pipeline in the reports and the people concerned with sales performance in your organization up to date.

You can easily do this by selecting a relevant stage from the *Stage* graph in the deal details page (Figure 4-49). In the graph, the current stage is shown as a green circle while previous stages are indicated as green check marks and future stages are grayed out. By default, the last three stages of a deal indicate if it is a win or a loss. Visually, these stages are indicated with thumbs-up or thumbs-down icons.

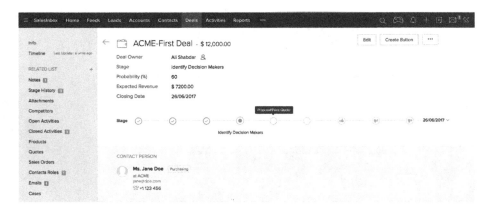

Figure 4-49. Moving a Deal along the sale funnel

To select an applicable stage, simply click on the next stage (gray circle) in line or jump and select another future stage. You can hover on a stage to see its name.

In an upcoming section, you will learn how to customize the deal stages to match your sales process.

Viewing Deals

To quickly see all active deals in the system in one place, click on *Deals* on the top menu bar. The *All Deals* view will show all deals grouped by stage (Figure 4-50). Click on each deal listed in the view to see its details.

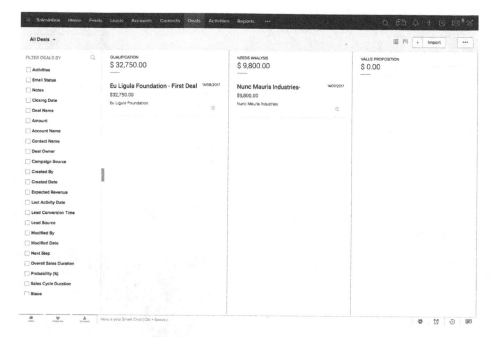

Figure 4-50. *Deals page with all deals listed in different stages of the pipeline*

All Deals view has two ways of displaying deals: one is the default-by-stage view, and the other is the simple list view. You can switch between these two by clicking on the *list* and *bar* icons on the top right of the screen.

Also, there are filters for you to select (from the left sidebar) to narrow down the list, in case there are many deals listed here. You can choose to see deals only for a specific account, stage, lead source, etc.

Similar to other modules, you can select other available views from the view selector drop-down on the top left of the screen and see, for example, only your own deals, deals closing this month, etc.

It is also worth reminding you that you can customize these views by clicking *Edit* next to the view selector drop-down and also create new views from scratch by clicking *Create New* item in the drop-down.

Homepage Dashboard

As you enter information in the CRM and keep it up to date, the homepage dashboard turns into a powerful place to quickly see the state of your business in one page.

By default, two of the four *Components* (what Zoho calls the building blocks of the dashboard page) show the list of the deals closing this month and the graph of the sales pipeline by stage, not surprisingly shaped like a funnel.

In Figure 4-51, you can see that there is only one deal closing this month and judging by the funnel, the majority of the deals are still in the qualification stage. Now, if this were a real business, you may have needed to ask the sales team some serious questions.

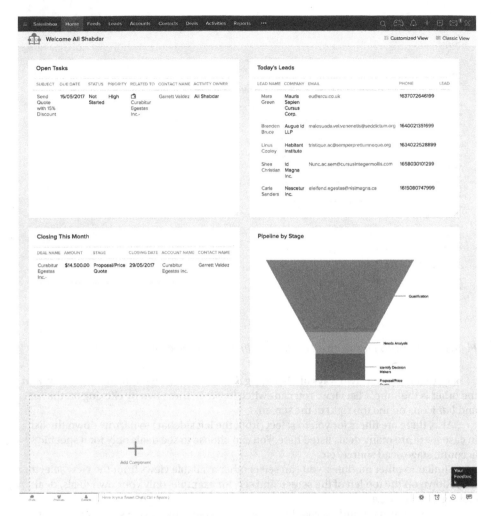

Figure 4-51. *Homepage dashboard showing the state of the business*

You can make the homepage more powerful and add more views and dashboards by clicking on the *Add Component* button (green plus sign) in the bottom of the page and choose from available views and dashboards in the CRM. I leave exploring this feature to you.

Customizing Stages

As you learned in a previous section, deals move forward in the pipeline from one stage to another until they are won or lost. Making sure deals are in the right stage will give you an accurate view of your business, so it is important to ensure these stages reflect your sales process correctly.

By default, Zoho provisions nine different stages in which a deal can be in: Qualification, Needs Analysis, Value Propositions, etc. You can modify the name of existing stages, add new ones, and remove the ones you don't need. Note that these customizations are global (i.e., organization wide) and will apply affect all deals in the CRM.

To customize the deal stages, follow these steps:

1. On the top bar, on the right, click on the tools icon, and then click on *Setup* (Figure 4-52).

Figure 4-52. *Opening the Setup page*

2. In the *Setup* page, under *Customization* group, click on Modules. A new page will open with all the CRM modules listed

3. In the modules list, hover the mouse cursor on *Deals*, click on the *(...)* button appearing next to *Deals*, and select *Stage-Probability Mapping* in the context menu (Figure 4-53).

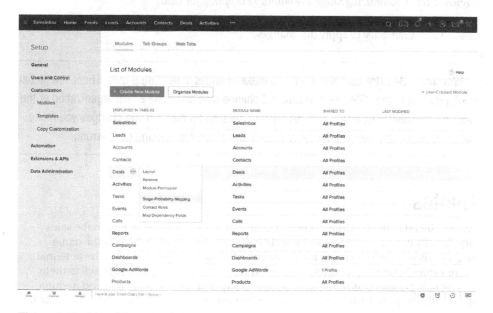

Figure 4-53. *List of CRM modules*

4. In the *Stage-Probability Mapping* dialog box, modify stage name, probability, forecast type, and forecast category for each stage you need to customize. Use the + and – buttons next to each stage to add a new stage or remove the respective stage (Figure 4-54).

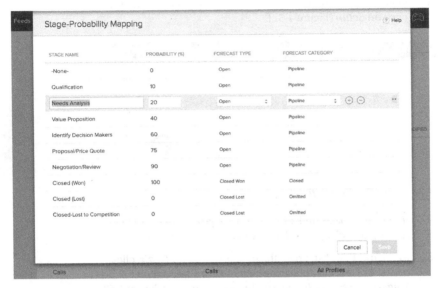

Figure 4-54. *Customizing Stage-Probability Mappings for deals*

5. Click *Save* to apply the changes.

■ **Warning** Be extra cautious when you make changes in the Setup area. These are global configurations of the CRM, and the smallest change may affect the entire organization or the data in a negative way. Make sure you back up data and remember the changes you make (takes notes, or screenshots), so you can undo the steps if something goes wrong.

Quotes

As mentioned in the previous section, a deal goes through various stages in the sales pipeline. By default, one of these stages is *Proposal/Price Quote*, which as the name suggests, is for when you reach a point in your deal that you need to send the potential (or returning) client a quotation for the products or services you intend to sell to them.

Sending quotations is a common stage in any deal. In fact, you may send multiple quotes with adjusted prices and terms, until the client is happy to proceed with the deal.

You can create quotes for an ongoing deal or directly in the Quotes module. I recommend the former, because it makes creating the quote easier and attaches it to the deal automatically.

Follow these steps to create a quote for a deal:

1. Open the deals module and open a deal.

2. In the deal detail page, click on Create + *New* under *Quotes* section (Figure 4-55).

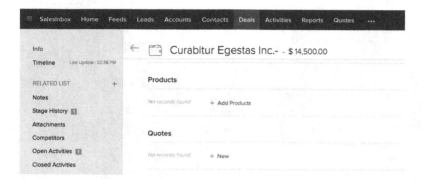

Figure 4-55. *Creating a quote for a deal*

3. In the *Create Quote* page, enter *Subject,* and V*alid Until* (Figure 4-56). Note that *Quote Owner, Quote Stage, Deal Name, Contact Name, Account Name,* and *Address Information* are prepopulated based on the deal information.

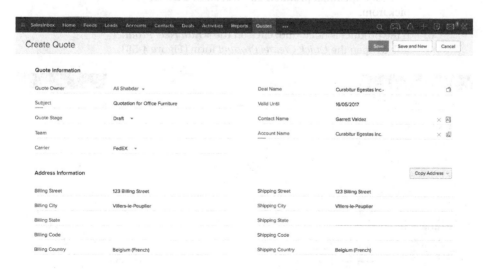

Figure 4-56. *Populating the new quote with quote and address information*

4. Under the *Product Details* section, click *Add Line Items*. A *Choose Products* form will open (Figure 4-57).

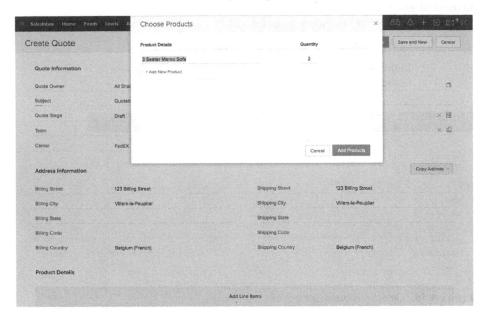

Figure 4-57. *Adding products to the quote*

5. In *Products Details*, type in the product name you want to add to the list. You can enter the product name partially. CRM will look for any similar products and will show a list for you to pick from.

6. If the product is not found, click on the *+ Add New Product* link to open the *Quick Create: Product* form (Figure 4-58).

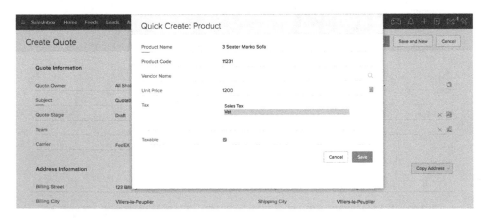

Figure 4-58. *Creating a new product on-the-fly for the quote*

7. In the quick create form, type in the product information as shown in Figure 4-58 and click *Save* when you are done.

8. Repeat from step 4 and create another product as shown in Figure 4-59. Click *Save* to continue.

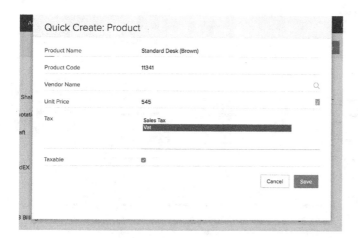

Figure 4-59. *Creating a second product on-the-fly*

9. Back in the *Choose Product* form (Figure 4-60) you have two products in the list. Click the *Add Products* button to continue.

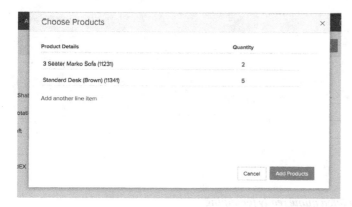

Figure 4-60. *Two newly created products ready to be aded to the quote*

10. The two products are added to the quote with the total amount of the quote calculated and placed nicely below the list items (Figure 4-61). As a last step, populate *Terms and Conditions* and click *Save* to create the quote.

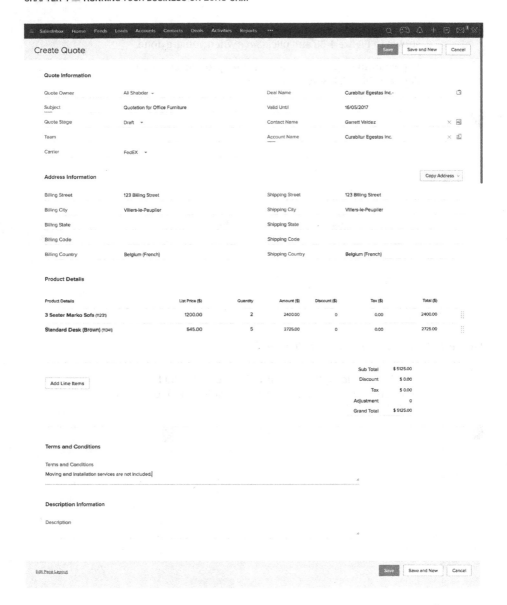

Figure 4-61. *A fully populated quote ready for saving*

The newly created quote will be listed under Quotes section in the deal details page (Figure 4-62). You can access the quote details or modify it from here. You can also add new quotes for the same deal.

Figure 4-62. New quote listed under Quotes in the deal page

Quotes are also accessible in the *Quotes* module. Click on *Quotes* on the top menu bar and a list of all quotes will be shown. You can click on each quote and see the details, modify, print, or export them to into PDF documents to send to concerned parties (Figure 4-63).

Figure 4-63. Details of the newly creted quote in the corresponding Quote page

Emailing Quotes

To send quotes to clients, you can export them to PDF and email them to clients and other people. You can also kill more trees and print them on paper to send them by snail mail (killing even more trees) or fax them if the other party lives in the previous century.

The better way, however, is to email quotes directly to the client (i.e., the contact mentioned in the quote) from within the CRM. To do this, follow these steps:

1. In the quote detail page, open the … menu on the top right of the screen and click *Send Mail* on the drop-down menu. The *Send Mail* form will open (Figure 4-64).

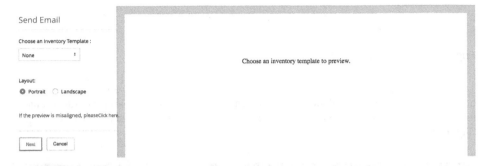

Figure 4-64. *Sending a quote (to a contact) via email*

2. Choose *Quote Template* from *Choose an Inventory Template* drop-down list. The quote will be formatted based on the template chosen and a preview will be displayed on the right side (Figure 4-65). Click *Next* to continue.

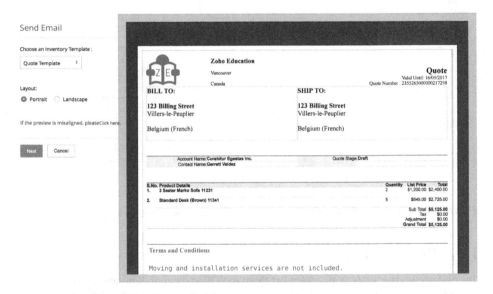

Figure 4-65. *Choosing a template for the quote*

3. The *Send Mail* window will load ready for you to populate the message body. To field is already populated from the quote contact and the quote itself is attached to the message (Figure 4-66).

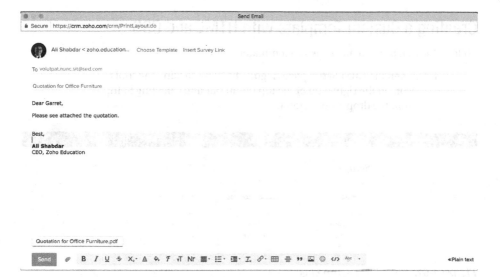

Figure 4-66. *Composing the email with the quote attached*

4. Click *Send* once you are happy with the message body. Your client will receive an email from you with the quote attached.

Customized Templates

In the previous section, you used a template for a quote. Templates in Zoho are predesigned pages that contain visual elements as well as placeholders for information to generate formatted output for quotes, invoices, emails, etc.

Templates help save time and also create a uniform way of generating output compliant with the branding guidelines of your business. For example, you can design templates that feature your logo and use your brand color and typeface while mentioning a generic note in the footer.

Then when you send documents such as quotes and invoices, they look professional and have the common elements across the board.

The template you used in the previous section was quite simple and unappealing at best. Apart from design, you may want to have different templates for quotes (or other modules) that have different elements in them.

Zoho CRM allows you to create complex templates with a great look and feel by simply using the template designer, dragging and dropping elements into the template. There is also a more advanced option for users who want full flexibility designing with HTML and CSS.

■ **Note** If you are not familiar with HTML and CSS, or not interested in designing Zoho CRM templates, now it's a good time to skip over to the next section.

Creating a Custom Template with HTML and CSS

Follow these steps to create a custom template:

1. Open the CRM *Setup* page (Figure 4-67) by clicking the tools icon on the right side of the top menu bar and selecting Setup from the drop-down menu.

Figure 4-67. Zoho CRM Setup page

2. In the *Setup* page, click on *Templates* under *Customization* section. The *Templates* page will open, listing the existing templates (Figure 4-68).

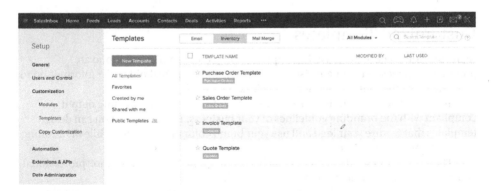

Figure 4-68. List of exisitng templates

3. There are three template categories: *Email*, *Inventory*, and *Mail Merge*. Click the *Inventory* button on top of the page to see a list of templates specifically designed for inventory-related templates such as quotes and invoices.

4.   While in the Inventory list, click the (blue) *New Template* button on the left side of the list.

5.   In the *Create Inventory Template* form (Figure 4-69), select *Quotes* for *Select Module* and click *Next*.

Figure 4-69. *Creating a new template for quotes*

6.   In the template designer page (Figure 4-70), click on the "<html>" icon (next to the smiley face) on the toolbar. Instead of using the rich text editor, we are going to paste some HTML code in here.

Figure 4-70. *Template editor*

7.   In your browser, open https://github.com/sparksuite/ simple-html-invoice-template (Figure 4-71). This is a modern and minimal invoice template you can use in your template and modify to your liking.

111

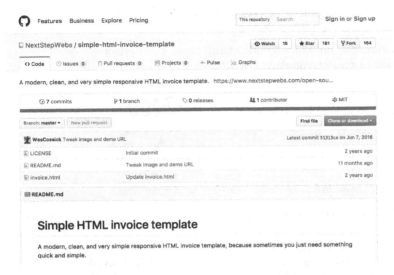

Figure 4-71. *Simple HTML Invoice Template page on Github*

8. In the file list on the page, click *index.html*. The source file will open (Figure 4-72).

Figure 4-72. *Simple HTML Invoice source code*

9. select all the HTML code, copy it, and paste it into the Edit HTML box in the CRM Template Editor you opened in step 6 (Figure 4-73).

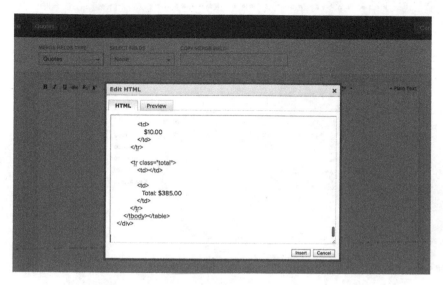

Figure 4-73. *Pasting the Simple HTML Invoice source code into the quote template HTML code*

10. Click *Insert* to continue. The template will be shown in the editor (Figure 4-74).

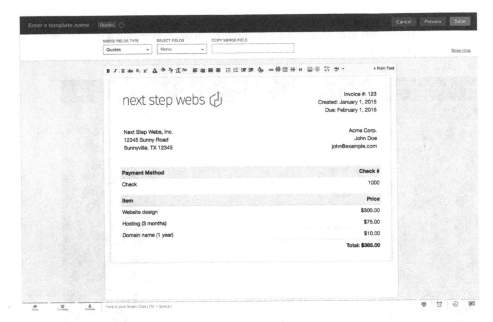

Figure 4-74. Simple HTML Invoice pasted as the quote template

11. To make the template work for you, add Merge Fields to its body, so these fields get replaced with real data relevant to a quote when a quote is generated (Figure 4-75). You can select the Merge Fields by selecting them from the two dropdowns on the top of the template deisgner and then copying and pasting the generated code in to the content.

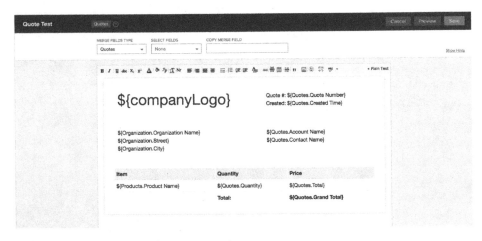

Figure 4-75. Customizing the quote template

12. Once you are done with designing the quote template, click the Save button. The template designer will close and you will be redirected to the list of existing templates (Figure 4-76). You can go back and edit these templates or create new ones for different purposes.

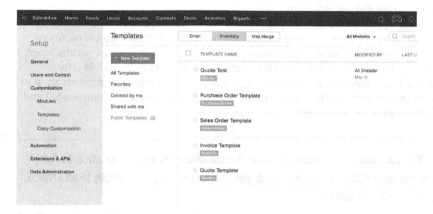

Figure 4-76. *New quote template appears in the list of Zoho CRM templates*

Figure 4-77 shows our newly created quote template in action. You can see that the merge fields are replaced with actual values from the quote.

Figure 4-77. *Using the new quote temaplate in action*

Converting Quotes to Sales Orders

A Sales Order (SO) is a confirmation document sent to the customer before delivering goods or services. In contrast, a Purchase Order (PO) is an order placed for procuring products or services from your vendors.

SO can be created once the quote is accepted by your customer often via a PO sent by the customer for further processing.

After sending your (the seller) the PO, the customers may request an SO to know the exact date of delivery of the goods or services. Also, the inventory/production department (if there is one) looks at the list of Sales Orders to see what needs to be shipped out and when.

Similar to quotes, you can create SOs directly in the *Sales Orders* module. The recommended way, however, is to convert a quote to an SO, so most of the information in the SO populates automatically from the quote and a logical connection between SO and other related documents is created.

■ **Note**   If in your business, creating SOs are not common and you create invoices right after a quote is accepted or a PO is received, you can convert a quote directly to an invoice, skipping the whole SO creation.

To convert a quote to an SO simply open it and click the (green) *Convert* button on the top of the quote details. Then select *Sales Order* from the drop-down menu (Figure 4-78).

Figure 4-78. *Converting a quote to a sales order*

Once the new SO is created it is displayed for you to review and perform other tasks on it. As you can see in Figure 4-79, the SO is quite similar to the corresponding quote as it gets its fields from the quote. However, there are subtle differences, such as the *SO Number* vs. *Quote Number*, *Status* vs. *Stage*, and the addition of *Sales Commission* field.

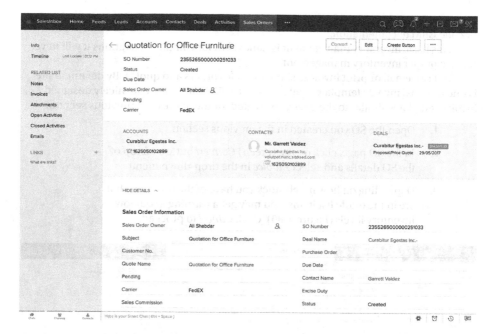

Figure 4-79. *Sales order details*

You can also see that there is a link to the corresponding quote and deal under *Sales Order Information* section, *Quote Name*, and *Deal Name*.

One more thing about the SO is to make sure you change the *Status* field as you go forward to reflect the actual status of the SO. As mentioned in the previous sections, you can change the values in the *Status* list in the *Setup* page under *Modules*.

Converting Sales Orders to Invoices

Once the sales stage reaches its final phase, you may start working on the payment procedure and, obviously, the invoice. This is an important stage for both sales and accounting purposes as it completes the sales process and begins the accounting process.

An invoice usually contains the PO reference number, date, address information, payment terms, line items (products/services) with quantities and prices as well as (optional) tax and discount information.

Again, you have the option of creating invoices from scratch, or converting a quote or SO to an invoice, bringing all the information from the base document.

Follow these steps to convert an SO to an invoice:

Not enough product in the inventory; go and change to 10 each; come back to sales order; convert.

Now if you go back to the Products page and check the Quantity in Stock, you will see that the number is changed to the balance of previous stock minus the number of products in the sales order.

You can add to the inventory either manually as you just saw, or through issuing POs.

Exercise: Order new products for the inventory by creating a new PO.

Hint: You will need to add a new Vendor to be able to issue a PO. If you get stock, refer to Zoho CRM documentation.[1]

This basic inventory management is handy, but for complex operations it will never replace proper inventory management.

You can email or print invoices similar to sales orders and quotes. By default, there is one minimal invoice template available in the CRM. You can create nicely designed invoice templates similar to the ones you created for the quotes in a previous section.

1. Open the SO you created in the previous section.

2. In the SO page, click on the (green) *Convert* button on top of the SO details and select *Invoice* in the drop-down menu.

3. Depending on how much stock you have of the products that are in the quote list items, you may get a warning about low inventory levels (Figure 4-80). Click *Cancel* to proceed.

Figure 4-80. *Converting a sales order to invoice interrupted, due to not enough stock of the inventory*

4. Open *Products* page (Figure 4-81) and find the products with a low quantity in the stock.

Figure 4-81. *List of Products*

___

■ **Note** By default the *All Products* view doesn't show the value of *Quantity in Stock*. You need to either check the products one by one, to see the quantity for each one, which is a pain; or you can quickly edit the view and add the extra column *Quantity in Stock* to it.

___

[1]https://www.zoho.com/crm/help/purchase-orders/

5. In the product details page change the *Quantity in Stock* value to an arbitrary number (because we are testing; otherwise this should match the real number in your inventory). Then click *Save* to apply the changes (Figure 4-82).

Figure 4-82. *Changing Quanitity in Stock for a product*

6. Now go back to the SO and convert it to an invoice. The invoice gets created immediately and you will be redirected to the invoice detail page (Figure 4-83).

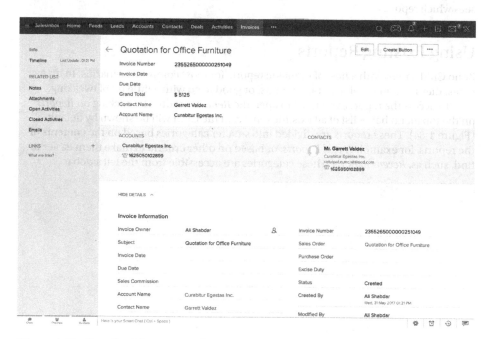

Figure 4-83. *Details of the converted invoice*

Take a moment and review the fields in the invoice. Many values are brought from the underlying SO (or quote, depending which one you converted).

Quite similar to quotes and SOs, you can print invoices, export them to PDFs, and send them via email to your clients directly from CRM.

Reports

You remember from the beginning of this chapter when we argued that one of the fundamental traits of good software is that you (the user) enters information once and then you can extract it by different means, each serving a specific purpose.

We have learned how to create leads, deals, quotes, etc., in Zoho CRM. We also learned that we can see this information through various avenues, by navigating through views and detail pages or searching through each module, or globally.

Zoho CRM provides yet another way of outputting information that it reports. Reports are read-only (you can't edit the data in a report), formatted, and often complex representation of the information in the CRM.

Similar to other entities, such as quotes and invoices, you can print, export, or email them. You can also define user-level and role-based access to the reports to specify who sees which report.

Using Existing Reports

Zoho CRM comes with a host of premade reports for most common scenarios. In many cases, they are quite usable out-of-the-box, or good to go with a little bit of tweaking.

To access the reports, you need to open the *Reports* module by clicking on *Reports* on the top menu bar. A list of all existing reports in the CRM will be shown by default (Figure 4-84). These reports are divided into smaller categories based on the contents of the reports, for example, *Lead Reports*; or based on other criteria to make them easier to find, such as, *Recent Reports*. These categories are accessible from the left sidebar.

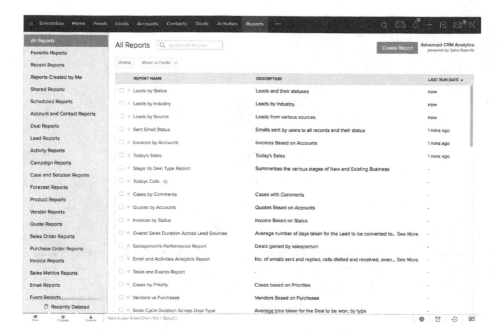

Figure 4-84. *List of default reports in Zoho CRM*

One nifty categorization is the *Favorite Reports*, which as the name suggests, allows you to group your favorite reports in one place.

To add a report to favorites, simply click on the gray star next to any report in the list, and the star will turn gold and the report will be added to the *Favorite Reports*.

Let's have a look at two of the available reports. The first one is *Leads by Status*, which shows all the leads grouped by their status (Figure 4-85). This report has two parts, a pie chart on the top providing a quick and visual representation of state of the leads in the organization, followed by a list of leads with more details and also grouped by the status.

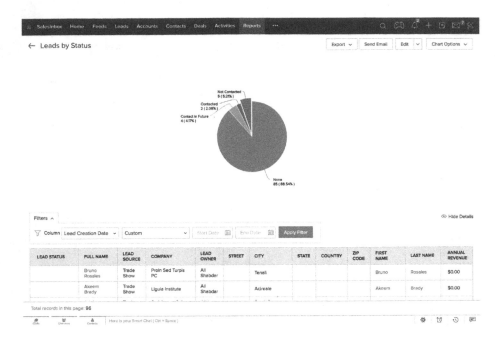

Figure 4-85. *Lead by Status Report*

The second one is *Pipeline by Stage*, which again is a two-part report with a funnel showing the volume of the deals in each stage of the pipeline on the top of the report. There is also a detailed list of pipeline stages and the deals in each stage, including the sum of the amount per stage (Figure 4-86).

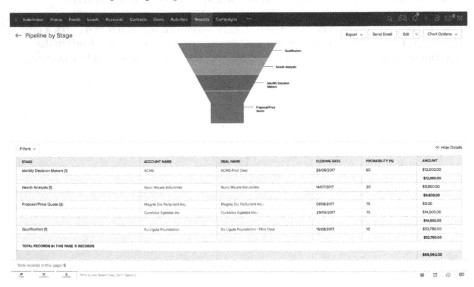

Figure 4-86. *Pipeline by Stage Report*

Creating New Reports

Of course, Zoho CRM comes with a collection of useful reports out-of-the-box that you can use or modify to your liking; however, there are times when you need to create a report from scratch. Thankfully CRM comes with a powerful report designer.

Follow these steps to create a new report from scratch:

1. Open the Reports page and click on the (green) *Create Reports* button on the top right of the list (Figure 4-87).

Figure 4-87. *Creating a new report – picking report type*

2. In the *New Report* wizard, start by setting module information and selecting *Deals* for the main module, and *Contact* and *Quotes* for related modules (Figure 4-88).

```
≡   SalesInbox   Home   Feeds   Leads   Accounts   Contacts   Deals   Activities   Reports   •••
```

New Report

1. Module Information

Select Module

[Deals   ⌄]

Select Related Modules

☑ Contacts
☐ Contact Roles
☐ Stage History
☐ Campaigns
☐ Products
☑ Quotes
☐ Sales Orders

[Continue]   [Cancel]

Figure 4-88. *Selecting the source modules for the new report*

3. Click Continue to proceed with *Report Type*. Select *Tabular Type* and click *Continue* (Figure 4-89).

Figure 4-89. *Selecting tabular format as the report type*

4. Under *Report Representation*, select the columns that will be showing in the report according to Figure 4-90. Then click *Continue*.

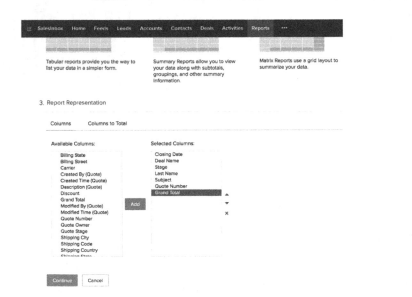

Figure 4-90. *Selcting information columns to show on the report.*

5. Under *Filters*, Select *Deal Closing Date* from the first drop-down, then *Current FY* in the second one, and set the date range to cover the current financial year (Figure 4-91). Click *Continue.*

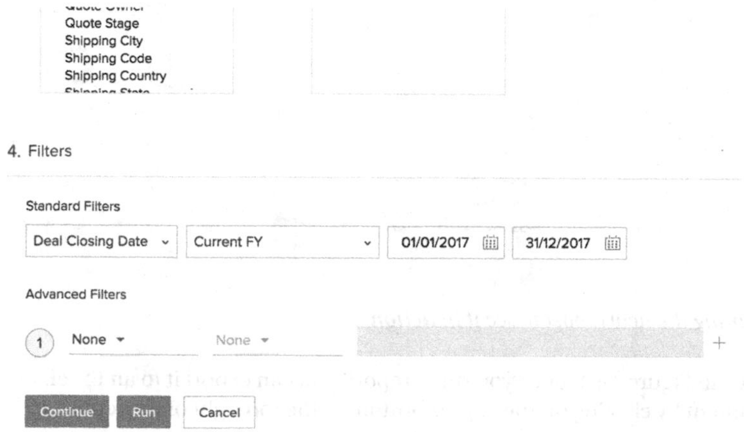

Figure 4-91. Setting a filter for the report.

6. Finally, under *Basic Information*, Select *Deal Reports* from the drop-down list, enter *"Deals and Quotes"* as the report name, and provide some description about what the report does (Figure 4-92).

Figure 4-92. Putting in report name and description

7. Click *Run* to see the report in action (Figure 4-93). If you like what you see click *Save*; otherwise click *Edit* to make changes in the report.

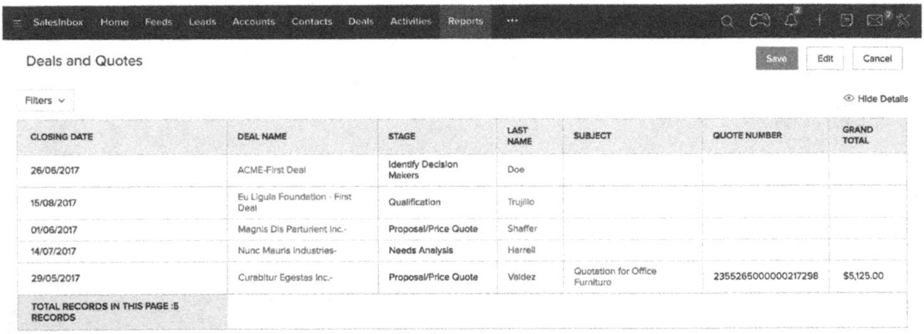

Figure 4-93. *Running the new report to see it in action*

As you can see in Figure 4-94, once you run a report, you can export it to an Excel, CSV, or PDF document by clicking on the *Export* button on the top right of the report.

Figure 4-94. *Options to export the report into different file formats*

You can also directly send out the report via email by clicking on the *Send Email* button.

Forecasting Your Business

One of the main reasons that you keep track of every movement in your business in the CRM is to be able to rely on the up-to-date key information and make successful tactical and strategic decisions toward the profitable and sustainable growth of your business.

One such piece of key information is the performance of your sales force and how close or far they are from hitting their targets. Setting clear, achievable, and yet ambitious sales targets allows you to plan for growth and budget for success, that is, depending on your strategic plans and projected sales, you allocate budget to areas that contribute to business growth and cut back on unnecessary costs.

Zoho CRM offers a Forecast module where you can, as the name suggests, forecast and also monitor the short-term and long-term sales performance of your business.

■ **Note** Getting into the details of business forecasting is beyond the scope of this book. We will be only scratching the surface by setting a simple forecast in Zoho CRM. If you have an (even small) sales force in your company and are serious about the growth of your business, I strongly suggest you learn more about business forecasting and also refer to Zoho CRM documentation on forecasting: https://www.zoho.com/crm/help/forecasts/.

Creating Your First Forecast

Let's start by creating a quarterly forecast for our sales team.

1. On the top menu bar, click on Forecasts. If this is your first time here, an introductory text will be shown about forecasting and its advantages for your business (Figure 4-95).

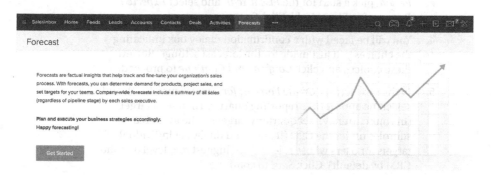

Figure 4-95. *Getting started with forecasting in Zoho CRM*

2. Click Get Started to continue. The *Forecast Settings* page will load asking you to enter settings for the new forecast (Figure 4-96).

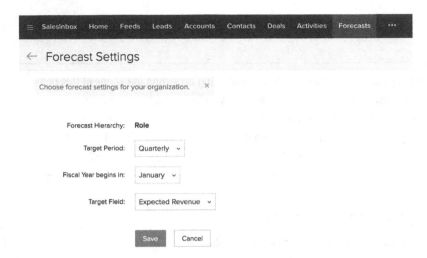

Figure 4-96. *Creating your first forecast*

3. In the *Forecast Settings,* page select *Quarterly* for *Target Period*, pick a start for the *Fiscal Year*, and select *Expected Revenue* for *Target Field*. Click Save to continue.

4. You will be faced with a confirmation dialog box indicating the choices you just made for the forecast settings. Review these choices and click *Confirm and Continue* to proceed.

5. In the next screen, *Create Forecast for CEO* (Figure 4-97), and select the appropriate reporting quarter. Then set a target (in your currency), set quarterly target for the available subroles under the CEO (if any), and finally set individual targets for users whose role is CEO (highest role level in Zoho CRM by default). Click *Save* to continue.

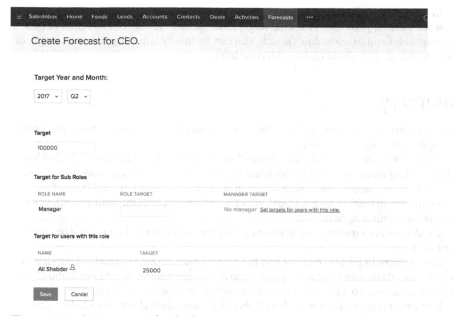

Figure 4-97. *Setting targets for the forecast*

6.   Immediately after the new forecast is created, the current state of your business in terms of role and individual performance will be reported in the *Forecast Summary* page (Figure 4-98).

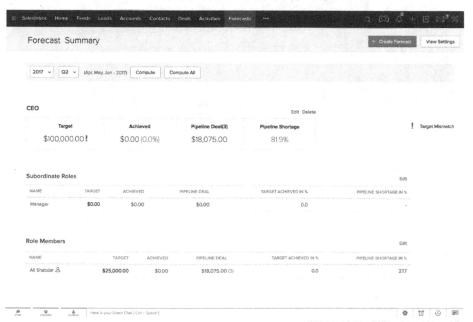

Figure 4-98. *Forecast Summary page*

In the summary page, you may see a red asterisk warning you about a mismatch in the target. This happens when the total target amount and the sum of individual targets for the subroles and its users don't match. You can fix this by adjusting the main target, or adding to the target amount of the team members.

Summary

This exhaustive chapter took you through the essential skills you need to run a successful sales operation using Zoho CRM.

You learned to start managing your sales force and processes with first managing leads and then taking them through the sales funnel, guiding them all the way to securing sales.

You learned about various modules, such as Accounts, Contacts, and Deals. You then continued to utilize Quotes, Sales Orders, and Invoices to communicate with your potential and returning customers.

We also covered reports and forecasting that are both essential for staying on top of your business.

This is a very important chapter and the learning will prove essential in your day-to-day business. Make sure you have a good grasp of all the topics covered here. Zoho CRM documentation[2] is also a good source of information for more in-depth help.

In the next chapter, we will see how Zoho CRM, with the help of other Zoho suite apps, can help you take control of all your marketing efforts.

---

[2]https://www.zoho.com/crm/help/

CHAPTER 5

■ ■ ■

Take Control of Marketing

In the previous chapter, we learned about managing the sales force and the pipeline. However, sales without marketing is like shooting in the dark. A big part of the success of any business depends on how it understands the target market and promotes its products and services to the right audience in the right time, and on the right promotional channels.

Zoho CRM offers a number of essential tools and features that help you stay on top of your marketing game without breaking the bank or going crazy managing a toolset of apps from different vendors. There are also a number of complementing Zoho apps that can greatly boost your CRM-centric marketing efforts.

Before delving into these tools, let's quickly touch on some of today's marketing challenges.

Marketing in the World of Micromoments

According to Dr. Philip Kottler, the father of modern marketing, "Marketing is the science and art of exploring, creating, and delivering value to satisfy the needs of a target market at a profit. Marketing identifies unfulfilled needs and desires. It defines, measures, and quantifies the size of the identified market and the profit potential. It pinpoints which segments the company is capable of serving best, and it designs and promotes the appropriate products and services".[1]

The core definition of marketing hasn't changed, but the tactics, methods, channels, and challenges are ever changing. With digital marketing taking over most of the marketing efforts of the modern businesses these days, it is very important to utilize the latest tools and trends to stay competitive in this noisy market.

In the recent years, mobile has been taking over as a major platform for people to interact online. People (in America) spend almost five hours on their phones every day,[2] and we can assume that the rest of the world are following suit.

The average attention span of the modern buyer is less than that of a goldfish (8.25 seconds, compared to 9 seconds, http://www.statisticbrain.com/attention-span-statistics/). This is impacted even more by hundreds of marketing messages and a million other distractions, such as messages and notifications on various devices that bombard people on a daily basis.

---

[1]http://www.kotlermarketing.com/phil_questions.shtml#answer3
[2]https://www.digitaltrends.com/mobile/informate-report-social-media-smartphone-use/

© Ali Shabdar 2017
A. Shabdar, *Mastering Zoho CRM*, DOI 10.1007/978-1-4842-2904-0_5

We, as a species, are struggling with unprecedented chronic information fatigue and it is only getting worse. So, it is important that you as a business get the most out of those precious seconds here and there that customers spend discovering, researching, or purchasing. These are called micromoments.

■ **Reference** Google, as the leading platform of digital marketing, has a fantastic collection of resources to learn more about the latest trends and best practices of content marketing called Think with Google. You can learn about micromoments and ways to turn those micromoments into successful marketing opportunities for your brand from `https://www.thinkwithgoogle.com/marketing-resources/micro-moments/`.

The marketing department of today needs, more than ever, to stay in constant touch with other parts of the business, especially sales and client servicing. It also needs to have access to an arsenal of tools to perform effective and efficient marketing.

Landing pages, email and social media campaigns, feedback collection, social listening, paid (digital) advertising, and other tools and platforms will help you better understand your market and tell your story better and to more people.

Campaign Management

Marketing activities often happen within a defined campaign. CRM Campaigns are often time bound and have clear objectives and are goal defined. They also have success measures defined and the performance of the campaign monitored.

Participating in a trade show, renting a booth in a mall, renting a billboard, and running an email campaign, all fit in the definition of a marketing campaign and can all be managed within Zoho CRM.

Creating Campaigns

Let's start learning about Zoho CRM campaign management features by creating our very first campaign.

1. On the top menu bar, click *Campaigns*. In the *Campaigns* page (Figure 5-1), click *Create Campaign* to continue.

Figure 5-1. Campaigns page opened for the first time

2. In the *Create Campaign* page (Figure 5-2), populate the campaign details. *Campaign Date* is the only mandatory field, but make sure you enter the *Start Date, End Date, Estimated Revenue,* and *Budgeted Cost* as every serious campaign needs to have this information in place.

Figure 5-2. *Creating a new campaign*

3. After entering campaign details, click *Save* to store the information. Then you will be redirected to the campaign details page (Figure 5-3).

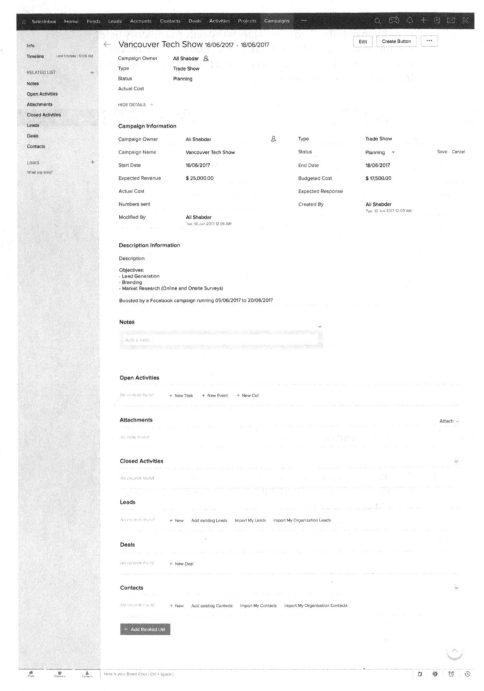

Figure 5-3. *Campaign detail page*

The campaign details page is quite similar to leads and contacts pages in terms of look and feel. You can add notes, tasks, and attachments to the campaign. You can also add leads, contacts, and deals to the campaign. We will learn more about this in a bit.

When you created the campaign the Status was set to *Pending* by default. Come back and update this field as you go forward with the campaign (Figure 5-4).

***Figure 5-4.** Changing campaign status*

Customizing Campaigns Module

Like any other standard module in Zoho CRM, you can customize the *Campaigns* module. You can add, edit, or remove fields to make the module match your business requirements.

In the next section, we will be adding leads already existing in the CRM to the campaign we just created. For that, we need a specific value to be set to a field called *Campaign Member Status*, which is not available in the preset values by default.

To fix this issue, we need to make a tiny change in the *Campaigns* module itself:

1. In Zoho CRM, open the *Setup* page by clicking on the Tool icon on the top menu bar and selecting Setup in the drop-down menu.

2. In the *Setup* page, under *Customization*, click *Modules*. A list of existing modules will be displayed.

3. Find *Campaigns* in the list and hover the mouse cursor on it. Then click the circular *(...)* icon appearing next to it (Figure 5-5) and click on *Campaigns Member Status* item in the drop-down list.

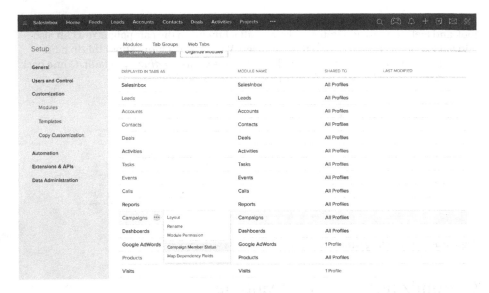

Figure 5-5. *Customizing the Campaigns module*

4. In the customization form (Figure 5-6), add *"Visited"* to the end of the list. This indicates that a person has visited our premises (or outlet) in person.

Figure 5-6. *Adding a new member status to Campaigns module*

5. Click *Save* to apply the changes and close the form.

Adding Leads to Campaigns

The main idea of running a campaign is to generate leads and turn them into paying customers down the road. To keep track of the leads generated from a specific campaign and then evaluate the performance of that campaign better, you can add leads, contacts, and deals to a campaign.

It is possible to add leads and contacts one by one, or add them in bulk from the leads already existing in the CRM. For deals, you can only add them one by one.

Suppose we have generated a number of leads, thanks to our recent participation in a trade show in Vancouver, BC. The leads are already in the CRM and now we need to add them to the campaign we created previously.

Follow these steps to add leads whose country is set to Canada to the campaign:

1. In the campaign details page, scroll down to the Leads section and click on the *Add Exiting Leads link*. The *Add existing Leads to Campaign* wizard will open (Figure 5-7).

Figure 5-7. *Adding existing leads to a campaign*

2. For the Criteria Component, select *"Country," "is,"* and type in *"Canada"* (Figure 5-8). Then click search to see the results, that is, the leads with the country field set to Canada.

	LEAD NAME	COMPANY	PHONE	EMAIL	LEAD STATUS	COUNTRY	CREATED TIME	LEAD OWNER
☐	Mara Green	Mauris Sapien Cursus Corp.	1637072646199	eu@arcu.co.uk	Contact in Future	Canada	15/05/2017 01:01 AM	Ali Shabdar
☐	Shea Christian	Id Magna Inc.	1658030101299	Nunc.ac.sem@cursusintegermollis.com	Contacted	Canada	15/05/2017 01:01 AM	Ali Shabdar
☐	Carla Sanders	Nascetur Inc.	1615080747999	eleifend.egestas@nisimagna.ca	Not Contacted	Canada	15/05/2017 01:01 AM	Ali Shabdar
☐	Xyla Collins	Id Enim Curabitur Foundation	1659062810299	quis@cursus.net	Contact in Future	Canada	15/05/2017 01:01 AM	Ali Shabdar
☑	Leandra Butler	Luctus Et Foundation	1697072929899	nulla@magnisdisparturient.org		Canada	15/05/2017 01:01 AM	Ali Shabdar
☑	Chiquita Mendez	Molestie Pharetra Nibh Foundation	1639121279299	rhoncus.id@penatibuset.com		Canada	15/05/2017 01:01 AM	Ali Shabdar
☑	Barbara Warren	Consequat Purus Company	1605012475199	tristique.pharetra@pellentesque.org		Canada	15/05/2017 01:01 AM	Ali Shabdar
☑	Deanna Cummings	Ullamcorper Incorporated	1699032403199	dolor@varius.edu		Canada	15/05/2017 01:01 AM	Ali Shabdar
☑	Xantha Malone	Elit Nulla Limited	1607112422099	volutpat.Nulla@acrisus.co.uk		Canada	15/05/2017 01:01 AM	Ali Shabdar
☑	Lacota York	Imperdiet Consulting	1660080497399	erat.nonummy@semelit.org		Canada	15/05/2017 01:01 AM	Ali Shabdar

Figure 5-8. *Selecting which leads to add to the campaign*

3. Select all or some of the leads in the result list. These selected leads will be added to the campaign.

4. Select *"Visited"* in the *Select Status* drop-down list. This value is what we just added to the *Campaigns* module in the previous section.

5. Click the *Add to Campaigns* button to proceed. You can see the selected leads are added to the campaign and the *Member Status* is set to *Visited* (Figure 5-9). These are the people who dropped by our stand in the trade show.

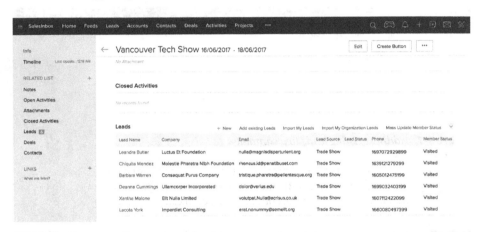

Figure 5-9. Leads added to the campaign

Webforms

Despite the ever-growing power of social networks, such as Facebook, the most effective marketing platforms remain emails.[3] The more you grow your email database, the more the chance of people seeing your message and acting upon it.

One of the most common ways of collecting email addresses and generating leads are HTML forms, often embedded in the contact or inquiry pages of websites. Sign-up forms that pop up on the screen or are placed in the footer of websites are also examples of webforms.

These forms collect the name, email address, and other information and send it back to marketers via email, saving in a database, pushing to email marketing services (e.g., Zoho Campaigns, MailChimp) or to CRM solutions (e.g., Zoho CRM, Salesforce).

---

[3]http://optinmonster.com/email-marketing-vs-social-media-performance-2016-2019-statistics/

Zoho CRM offers an intuitive way to generate forms and embed them into your website to collect information from the visitors. This information can then be pushed automatically to Leads, Contacts, Cases, or any custom module created in Zoho CRM for storing and further processing.

Creating a Webform

To have a form on your website that automatically pushes information collected on your site back to the CRM, first you need to create a webform in the CRM.

Suppose we need a simple form on our e-commerce site that collects visitors' basic information to sign them up for our monthly special offer newsletter. Follow these steps to create a webform for this purpose:

1. Open Zoho CRM *Setup* page. Under *Extensions & APIs*, click on *Webforms*. The *Webforms* page opens waiting for you to create your first webform (Figure 5-10).

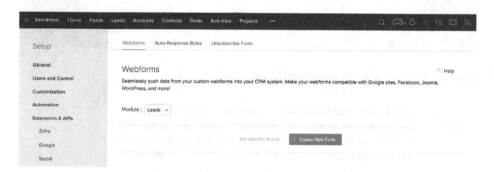

Figure 5-10. *Leads added to the campaign*

2. Make sure the *"Leads"* module is selected in the drop-down list and then click the click *Create Webform* button. The webform designer opens (Figure 5-11).

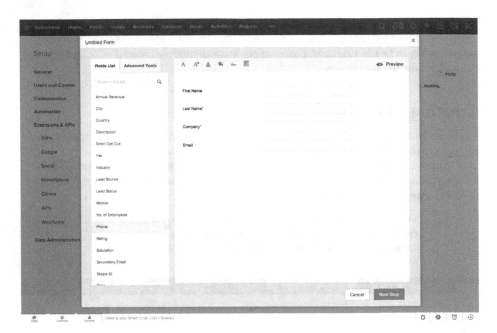

Figure 5-11. *Designing the form in Webform designer*

3. The designer adds two fields to the form by default: *Last Name* and *Company*. Add two more fields: *First Name* and *Email*, by dragging them from the fields list on the left sidebar and dropping them on the form in the order you see above.

4. Hover the mouse cursor on the *Email* field and click on the gear icon that shows up next to it (Figure 5-12).

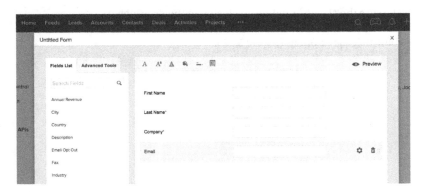

Figure 5-12. *Changing the settings of the Email field*

5. In the *Field Properties* dialog box, tick the *Mark as required field* check box to make Email a mandatory field on the webform (Figure 5-13). Click *Done* to get back to the webform designer.

Figure 5-13. *Making Email field mandatory*

6. Similarly, open *Field Properties* for the *Company* field and remove the required field check mark (Figure 5-14). Click *Done* to get back to the webform designer.

Figure 5-14. *Making Company field optional*

7. Add a new field *Lead Source* to the bottom of the form. We don't want visitors to see this field. Instead, we need this field to set a value to the lead (in CRM) without user input. So, we should hide this field.

8. Open *Field Properties* for *Lead Source* (Figure 5-15). Tick *Mark as hidden field* and set the *Default Value* to *Online Store*. Click *Done* to get back to the webform designer.

Figure 5-15. *Making Lead Source field hidden*

9. Back in the webform designer feel free to use formatting tools available via icons on top of the form to change fonts, colors, etc. (Figure 5-16).

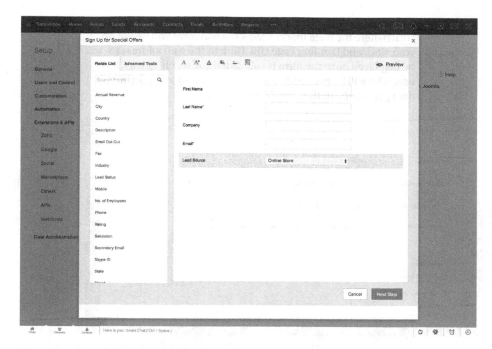

Figure 5-16. *Webform design completed*

10. Click on the Preview link on the top right of the designer to see how your webform will look like in action (Figure 5-17). Close the preview when you are done reviewing the form.

Figure 5-17. *Previewing the webform*

11. When you are happy with the webform, click *Next Step* to continue.

12. In the Form Details page, enter Form Name, Form Location URL (where the page that contains the webform will reside on your site), and Landing Page URL (link to the web address to be displayed once the form is submitted). Also, choose a CRM user who will be assigned as the lead owner once the form data gets stored in the CRM (Figure 5-18).

Figure 5-18. *Setting webform behavior*

13. Under *Notification*, enable *Notify Lead Owner* and leave *System Generate Mail* selected. Also, enable *Acknowledge Visitor* to send them an acknowledgment email once they submit a form. Select *Choose a default response for all visitors* (Figure 5-19).

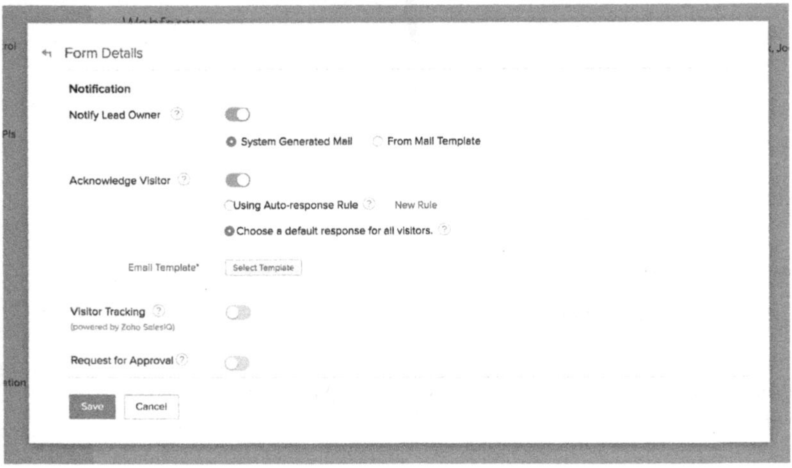

Figure 5-19. *Setting webform behavior*

14. Click on *Select Template* to choose an email template for the default response that will be sent to visitors. The *Select Template* window opens with no templates to choose from (Figure 5-20). Click on *Create Template* on the bottom.

If you have a template to pick, skip to step 23.

Figure 5-20. No email templates to pick from

15. The Zoho CRM email template gallery will open in a new window (Figure 5-21). Here you can choose from a collection of email ready-made templates and modify them to your liking.

Figure 5-21. Email template gallery

16. In the template gallery, click on *Notification* category on the left sidebar and choose a notification template. Click *Select* as your choice to continue. The template opens in a template designer ready for you to take an artistic stab on it (Figure 5-22).

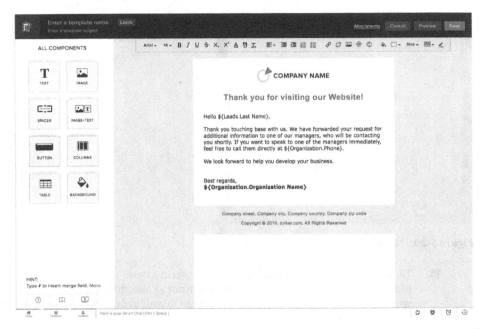

Figure 5-22. *Customizing the selected email template*

17. Click on the logo image on top of the template to change it to your organization logo. *Image Selection* dialog box opens, allowing you to choose a logo image (Figure 5-23). Click *Insert* when you are finished.

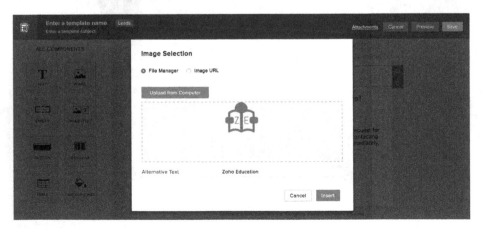

Figure 5-23. *Replacing the logo on the template*

146

18. Click on the body of text below the main title (Figure 5-24). You can edit the content and add merge fields to the text. Merge fields allow you to send more personalized emails by extracting personal information of the lead, such as first name (formatted as "*${Leads. First Name}*") and placing in the email body for every email sent out.

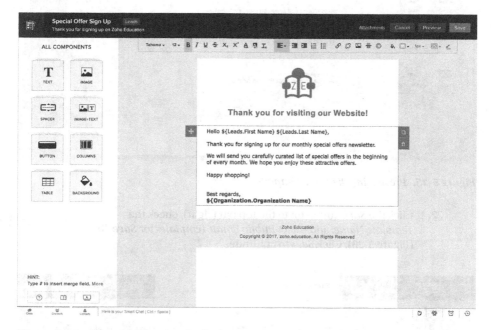

Figure 5-24. *Changing the message body*

19. Feel free to change the fonts, colors, and other design elements of the email template using the toolbar placed on top of the designer window.

20. You should name your email template and set an email subject to it too. Click on the corresponding placeholders on top bar (left) of the designer and type in the name and the subject.

21. When you are finished designing, click *Preview* on the top bar to see what your masterpiece will look like when received by the lead (Figure 5-25). Of course, those weird merge tags will be replaced by real values coming from the lead. You can click *Send Test Mail* to receive a copy of the email in your inbox for further reviewing. Then close the preview.

Figure 5-25. *Previewing the email template*

22. Click the *Save* button on to the top bar (right), check the *Template Name,* and select *Public Email Templates* for *Save To* (Figure 5-26). Click *Save* to continue.

Figure 5-26. *Saving the email template*

23. Go back to Select Template screen and click the little Refresh button appearing there. The newly created template will show up in the list (Figure 5-27). Click on the template to select it.

Figure 5-27. *New template shows up in the templates list*

24. On the Form Details screen, you can see the email template is selected (Figure 5-28). Review the email address mentioned in the *From* field and click *Save* to continue.

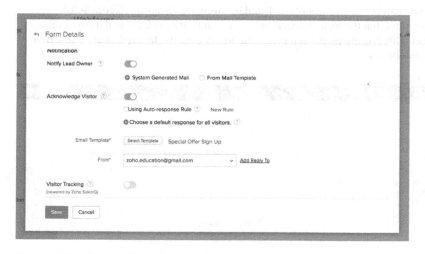

Figure 5-28. *Done with the form configuration*

25. On the *Embed options* screen, select the code you prefer to use to embed the webform into a webpage on your site (Figure 5-29). Consult with a web developer if you have no clue what that gibberish code is. Click *Done* to finish the process.

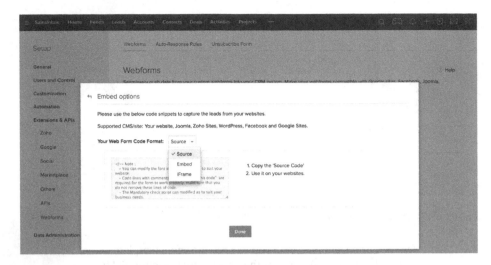

Figure 5-29. *Getting the HTML source code of the webform*

Now you can see the new webform listed in the *Webforms* page (Figure 5-30). The Status shows that the form is active. You can deactivate the form and it won't take information. This is quite useful as it gives you power over the forms that are published on external websites.

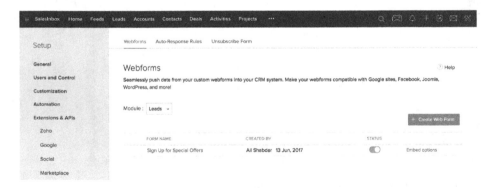

Figure 5-30. *Newly created webform listed and active*

To access the form embed code at any time in the future, you can click on *Embed options*.

Mass Email

One of the key features of Zoho CRM is that you can send emails from within the CRM and also keep a track of them too. For instance, you can perform the entire email correspondence with a lead right from the lead details page itself.

However, sometimes you need to send an email to a group of people at once. For instance, you may want to send a public announcement about your holiday hours to your contacts, or send a limited offer to your contacts.

For such scenarios, Zoho CRM offers a mass email feature, which allows you to send hundreds of emails to a select group of leads or contact at once.

This useful feature saves you a lot of time and also allows you to set up scheduled email dispatches and the possibility that your recipients can opt-out from future communications.

■ **Note**   There is a limit to how many emails you can send per day to your leads and contacts. See `https://www.zoho.com/crm/help/email/mass-email.html` to check the current limits for your edition of Zoho CRM.

It is worth mentioning that although the mass email feature of Zoho CRM is quite useful in many scenarios, if you want to get serious about email marketing and send thousands of emails to different people and monitor the performance of your email campaigns among other things, you need a full-fledged email marketing service, such as Zoho Campaigns. We will have a quick look at this service later in this chapter.

Sending Mass Emails

For now, let's try the mass email feature by sending a promotional email to all of our leads:

1.   Open the *Leads* page. Open the ... menu on top of the leads list and select Mass Email (Figure 5-31).

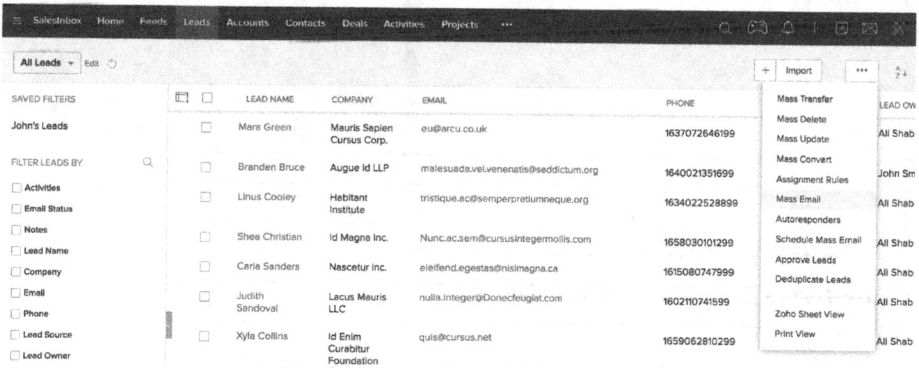

Figure 5-31. *Sending mass emails to leads*

2.   In the Mass Email wizard (Figure 5-32), review the information about email sending limits and spamming considerations.

151

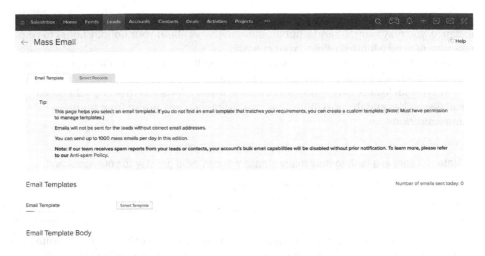

Figure 5-32. *Mass Email wizard*

3. Click the *Select Template* button under *Email Template* section.

4. In the *Select Template* screen (Figure 5-33), select an email template. Create a new template if you need one.

Figure 5-33. *Selecting an email template*

5. Once you select an email template, it will be previewed (Figure 5-34). Review the template and set the *From* field to the right CRM user.

Email Templates

Number of emails sent today: 0

Email Template

Select Template   Complementary First Consultation

From

Record Owner's Email   ▼   Add Reply To

Email Template Body

Figure 5-34. *Rviewing the template and setting the email sender*

6. Choose the second tab, Select Record, to specify the recipients of the mass email.

7. Under *Specify Criteria*, select *Custom View Criteria* and pick *My Leads* from the drop-down list. A list of all leads in *My Leads* view will be listed (Figure 5-35).

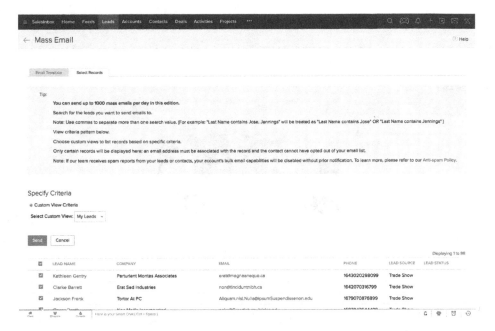

Figure 5-35. *Selecting the target leads*

8. Select all or some of the leads in the list. Then click on the *Send* button and proceed with confirmation to send the mass email. Et voilà!

After a few moments (depending on how many emails are being sent), you will be receiving a confirmation message informing you about the number of emails sent successfully (Figure 5-36).

Figure 5-36. *Sucessful email dispatch confirmation*

Sending Schedules Mass Email

As mentioned before, you can also schedule mass emails to be sent on a specific date and time in the future. This is quite similar to the previous section, so I leave exploring it to you.

Feel free to refer to the official documentation if you get stuck: https://www.zoho.com/crm/help/email/mass-email.html#Schedule_Mass_Email.

Zoho CRM for Google AdWords

Google AdWords® is the Holy Grail on online advertising outside of social networks, especially if you want to advertise on Google search and a Google network of partners.

Zoho CRM integrates well with Google AdWords to offer you a better understanding of possible connections between online marketing efforts and offline customer interactions with your business, such as calling in, buying, or visiting your outlet.

This integration also helps with fine-tuning your AdWords campaigns by exporting information from CRM to AdWords.

It is safe to assume that not all readers utilize Google AdWords. Those who do either have an in-house skillset to work with the complexities of AdWords, or they outsource talent to do the same.

In either case, we are going to skip delving into this integration and leave it to experts who are in charge of your AdWords campaign. Just make sure that you refer to Zoho official documentation at `https://www.zoho.com/crm/help/google-adwords/` before.

Zoho Suite Marketing Arsenal

Apart from the essential marketing tools and features offered in the CRM, Zoho suite offers three more apps that each cover a major part of digital marketing.

In the beginning of this book, *Zoho Suite from 10,000 feet*, we mentioned the name of these apps. In this section, we will have a super quick view at how each one of these apps integrates with Zoho CRM and extends its marketing capabilities.

Email Marketing with Zoho Campaigns

Based on personal experience and recent reviews, Zoho Campaign is quickly becoming one of the best email marketing tools for SMEs finding its place among the household names, such as MailChimp.

It also integrates well with Zoho CRM. An added bonus is that you get to enjoy the single sign-on to Campaigns, CRM, and all other Zoho apps.

You can import existing leads and contacts from CRM into Campaigns and add them to mailing lists. You can then send emails to these lists and enjoy the advanced reporting features of Zoho Campaigns to evaluate how successful your campaign has been.

Zoho Campaign also allows you to set up sign-up forms to be embedded in the websites to generate leads. You can export these newly generated leads back to CRM.

By enabling two-way periodic syncing, you can configure Campaigns in a way that acts as an extension to CRM. With the CRM at the center of your of your sales force automation, Campaigns can add a lot of value to your marketing efforts.

■ **Reference**   Zoho Campaigns is a full-fledged email marketing app worth learning about and using in your business, especially if you are a Zoho CRM user. Refer to official documentation to learn more about Zoho Campaigns: `https://www.zoho.com/campaigns/help/` and `https://www.zoho.com/campaigns/help/integrations/zoho-apps.html#Integrate_Zoho_CRM`.

Managing Social Media Channels with Zoho Social

With all the craziness in the social media space and the multitude of outlets for the marketers (or marketing departments) to take care of, social media management tools have become a de facto part of a marketer's toolbox.

Zoho Social is becoming a contender in this crowded space. Offering many useful features while being competitively priced, and also integrating well with Zoho CRM, Zoho Social is well worth the investment.

The integration enables a host of useful features, such as helping you stay engaged with your clients and prospect on social media, and creating leads from your social conversations and interaction with prospects on social media. You can even automate some activities, setting Zoho Social to turn new "likes" or "retweets" on social media automatically into leads on CRM.

■ **Reference**   Zoho Social is a full-fledged social management app worth learning about and using in your business, especially if you are a Zoho CRM user. Refer to official documentation to learn more about Zoho Social: `https://www.zoho.com/social/help/`; `https://www.zoho.com/social/help/integration-zoho-crm.html`; and `https://www.zoho.com/social/zohocrm-integration.html`.

Collecting Customer Feedback with Zoho Survey

If you remember from Chapter 2, the CRM triangle consists of marketing, sales, and customer service. All three of these require staying engaged with clients and prospects alike. No matter how happy or unhappy a client is, their feedback is always golden for the success of the business.

Zoho Survey is a powerful tool that helps you interact with clients and prospects by asking them key questions about their preferences, experience, feedback, etc. The output of such surveys could be invaluable for your sales force and other team members.

With Survey integrated with CRM, your team can see the results of surveys in real time, sync survey responses back to CRM, and view responses in customer contexts.

■ **Reference**   Zoho Survey is a full-fledged survey management app worth learning about and using in your business, especially if you are a Zoho CRM user. Refer to official documentation to learn more about Zoho Survey: `https://www.zoho.com/survey/help/`; `https://www.zoho.com/survey/help/integrations.html#integrate-with-zoho-crm`; and `https://www.zoho.com/survey/crm-integration.html`.

Summary

In this chapter, you learned about the marketing automation features of Zoho CRM: campaigns, webforms, and mass email. There was also an honorable mention of scheduled mass emails and integration with Google AdWords.

We also touched on other Zoho suite apps that integrate with CRM and extend its marketing capabilities: Zoho Campaigns, Zoho Social, and Zoho Survey.

In the next chapter, we will discuss in detail how Zoho CRM integrates with other Zoho apps as well as some useful external services to go beyond just being a CRM for your business.

CHAPTER 6

■ ■ ■

Integrating CRM with Zoho Ecosystem

In the previous chapter, we quickly touched on how we can extend capabilities of Zoho CRM by integrating it with other Zoho apps. For instance, by integrating CRM with Zoho Campaigns you can use the power of a robust email marketing tool to engage with your prospects and your customers.

The previous chapter was solely focused on marketing and integrating with apps that can boost your marketing efforts. Similarly, you can connect Zoho CRM to other apps in Zoho suite and extend its capabilities in different areas, such as finance, project management, and document management.

Easy integration and single sign-on (log in once and use all Zoho apps with the same account) is arguably one of the differentiating factors of the Zoho suite, thanks to a collection of interoperating business apps.

In this chapter, we will have a quick look at other Zoho apps that can improve your productivity and make your life easier by connecting to Zoho CRM. I won't be getting into details about any of these apps and assume that you (or people in your team) either have a basic idea of how each of these apps works, or you are planning to learn more about them. Otherwise integrating them with Zoho CRM will be pointless.

■ **Note** Zoho CRM also integrates with a myriad of third-party apps and services, including Google Apps, Microsoft Office, MailChimp, and SurveyMoneky (see the full list here: https://www.zoho.com/crm/integration/). The focus of this chapter is integrating with Zoho apps. We will quickly touch on third-party integrations in the next chapter.

All the Zoho Integrations

Zoho CRM can easily integrate with these Zoho apps:

- Zoho Mail – to bring emails into CRM and stay in touch with clients and prospects more effectively;

- Zoho Campaigns – to plan and execute successful email campaigns directly from CRM and generate detailed analytics;

- Zoho Reports – to generate sophisticated enterprise-level business reports and analytics;

- Zoho Survey – to run surveys and link results directly to CRM;

- Zoho SalesIQ – to bring the valuable data from your website visits and visitor interactions into CRM;

- Zoho Projects – to manage all your projects from the comfort of the CRM;

- Zoho Desk – to provide better support to your customers inside CRM;

- Zoho Writer – to improve productivity features of CRM, such as mail merge;

- Zoho Finance Suite– to stay on top of your accounting by connecting bookkeeping and accounting apps to CRM;

- Zoho Creator – to dramatically extend capabilities of CRM by creating fully customized and integrated business applications; and

- Zoho Motivator – to turn selling into engaging and rewarding games for your sales force.

One key point to keep in mind is that these integrations are between CRM and other Zoho apps that each offer limited free service and different tiers of paid services, each unlocking a different set of features. You may need to pay extra for each integrating app to keep certain features available beyond the (often 15-day trial period).

Now let's have closer at these integrations. We have already looked at Zoho Campaigns and Survey in Chapter 5. Here, we will have a closer look at integration with Zoho Mail, Projects, Invoice, Books, and Creator. You can explore other apps and integration as you wish.

■ **Note**   Your Zoho account must have an Administrator level account for you to be able to configure integrations.

Integrating with Zoho Mail

In Chapter 3, you have configured email for CRM and enabled Sales Inbox. That was actually your first integration of an external service, that is, email with CRM. By doing so, CRM and your email account are connected to each other and exchange information to give you a better idea about your day-to-day business.

For instance, the moment you connect your (work) email address to CRM, the email history of your contacts will appear in their corresponding contact detail page. You can send emails directly from the contact page and they will appear in your sent items as if they were sent from your email client (e.g., Zoho Mail, Outlook, Apple Mail).

■ **Note** Regardless of the email service you are using, be it Zoho, Gmail, Outlook, or others, Zoho Mail is the email client (or, email app) that manages your email account from Zoho or other services. So, if you have an @zoho.com, @gmail.com, or @yourcompany.com email address, you configure Zoho Mail to be your email app and that is what actually integrates with Zoho CRM.

Sharing Emails with Other CRM Users

There is one more feature that you can use to enable emails in the CRM, which is the ability to share all or some of your emails with other CRM users. Depending on your business process and internal policies, you have the option of letting other users see your email correspondence with your leads and contacts.

For example, sometimes your superior officer may need to see past communications without asking you to be bothered with forwarding messages to them. They can simply take a peek at your emails directly.

Now, this may sound creepy, or even unnecessary, but there are scenarios where this feature comes in handy. Obviously, other email messages in your inbox that have nothing to do with leads or contact in the CRM will not be shared with others even if email sharing is on for your account. Phew!

By default, email sharing is off, which means all your email correspondence is only visible to you. An administrator or the users themselves can change this setting.

There are three types of email sharing available:

- *Complete*: all the emails of the sharing user will be accessible to the users specified,

- *Custom*: sharing user will decide which email to share with whom, and

- *Private*: no emails will be shared: default state.

Follow these steps to adjust the email sharing settings:

1. In Zoho CRM Open the Setup page, then click Email Settings under Generic section.

2. On the *Email Settings* page, open the *Email Sharing* tab. Under *Email Sharing Permissions* there is a list of all users with their email sharing status in front of them, *Private* for the CEO and *User's Choice* for the rest (Figure 6-1).

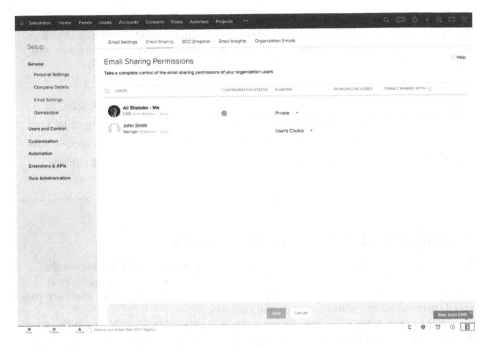

Figure 6-1. *Email Sharing tab in the Email Settings page*

3. Click on the status of the *CEO* (you) and select *Custom* from
    the drop-down list. Notice the value *Emails Shared With*
    column in the list column changes to *All* (Figure 6-2). This
    essentially means that this user's emails are now shared with
    everybody, which is not optimal and needs to be limited.

Figure 6-2. *Changing email sharing settings for a user.*

4. Click on the value *All* in the list. The *Email Sharing Setting*
    dialog box for the user opens (Figure 6-3). A series of selected
    check boxes will be listed showing the hierarchy of roles in
    your organization down to the users.

Figure 6-3. *Selecting email sharing permissions from existing roles and users*

5. Uncheck *All,* so all check boxes are unchecked. Then select which roles or users you want to permissions to. Click *Done* to proceed.

6. *Emails Shard With* value is now changed to a more limited and certain number of roles and users (Figure 6-4).

Figure 6-4. *Custom email sharing applied*

■ **Reference** Review details of email sharing permission in the official documentations: https://www.zoho.com/crm/help/zoho-mail/email-sharing.html.

Integrating with Zoho Projects

Projects are commonplace in most businesses and managing projects often needs a dedicated tool. Simpler projects, such as renovating the office flooring, can be easily managed with a to do list app, or an Excel sheet, but as projects grow, the number of tasks, interdependencies, priorities, project team, and stakeholders will grow too. In such case, starting off with a reliable project management app is a prudent move.

For those of us who use Zoho CRM, the good news is that you can use Zoho Projects alongside CRM and integrate them to make things easier for your team and your client.

In an ideal scenario, you start with a lead in the CRM, convert it into a deal, and take it through the pipeline until you close a deal.

Suppose you are a service provider, say a web design agency that uses Zoho CRM for sales force automation. When you win a deal, it means a new project kicks off with all the bells and whistles. You can easily create a project from within CRM, assign team members, track billable hours, monitor project performance, and stay in touch with the client, all from the same place.

By default, CRM adds a link to projects portal in the top menu bar. To set up the integration, follow these steps:

1. In Zoho CRM, open the *Projects* page and then click on the *Get Started* button (Figure 6-5). Alternatively, you can open *Setup* ➤ *Extensions & APIs* ➤ *Zoho* ➤ *Zoho Projects* (Figure 6-6).

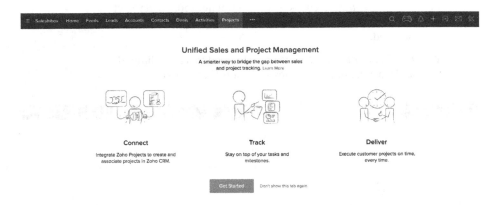

Figure 6-5. *Setting up CRM and Project intregation directly from the Projects page*

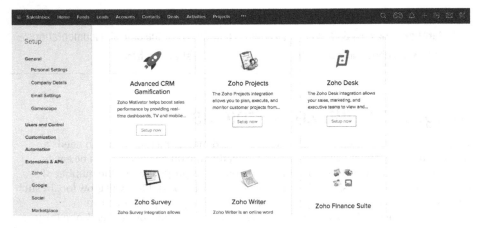

Figure 6-6. *Setting up CRM and Project intregation from the Setup page*

2. If this is your first time using Zoho Projects, you may get a warning message: "*Client Mapping: No client account found to match.*" Ignore this and proceed.

3. In the Zoho Projects Integration page (Figure 6-7), select *Create New Portal* to continue.

Figure 6-7. *Setting up Zoho Projects for the first time*

1. In the *Portal Configuration* step (Figure 6-8), type in a *Portal Name*. This name needs to be a single word with no space and special characters in it. Click *Create* to continue.

Figure 6-8. *Setting a portal name for Zoho Projects*

2. Next, under Choose Portal, select the portal you created in the previous step from the drop-down list (Figure 6-9).

Figure 6-9. *Selecting the newly created Projects portal to be integrated with CRM*

3.   We will have to give permission to CRM users to access Projects. There are five different permissions to grant to users: to see Projects tab (page) in the CRM, view projects, create projects, edit projects, and delete projects. Grant Administrators access permission to all these by ticking the corresponding check marks. Then grant only *Tab Visibility* and *View* to *Standard* users (Figure 6-10).

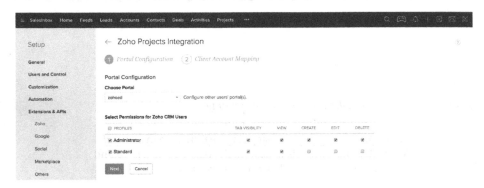

Figure 6-10. *Granting permissions to CRM users to access different aspects of Projects*

4.   Click *Next* to finish the integration. Then review the settings and permissions and edit them if necessary by clicking on the *Edit Configuration* link (Figure 6-11).

Figure 6-11. *Reviweing the intregation settings after a sucessful connection*

5.   To test the integration open the *Projects* page in the CRM. You will be welcomed by a warning page (Figure 6-12) saying that you are yet to create a project. Click on the *New Project* button, if you wish to continue with *Zoho Projects* at this point.

Figure 6-12. *Oops, no projects yet*

■ **Reference** If you get stuck somewhere, feel free to refer to the official documentation at `https://www.zoho.com/crm/help/zoho-projects/activate-zoho-projects-integration.html`.

Integrating with Zoho Finance Suite

Arguably, CRM (any flavor) and financial software (accounting, bookkeeping, etc.) are two of the most important information systems (or software) any organization can have in their arsenal.

So, it is safe to say that in most cases, if not all, having them work together under one roof would sound like a very good idea. Fortunately, if you are a Zoho user, you can integrate Zoho CRM and *Zoho Finance Suite* (*Books, Invoice, Expense, Subscriptions*) and have them work together.

Follow these steps to integrate Zoho CRM and Zoho Finance Suite:

1. In Zoho CRM open *Setup* ➤ *Extensions & APIs* ➤ *Zoho* ➤ *Zoho Finance Suite*. Then click on the *Get Started* button in the integration page (Figure 6-13).

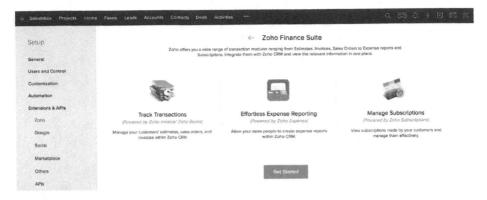

Figure 6-13.

2. In the next page (Figure 6-14), select the Finance Suite apps that you want to integrate with CRM and then click *Next* to continue.

Figure 6-14. *Selecting Finance Suite apps to integrate with CRM*

3. The page expands. Enter organizational details of your company similar to Figure 6-15. This information will be used by the Finance Suite apps selected in the previous step to create an organization. Click *Next* when you are done.

Figure 6-15. *Entering organizational details*

4. The page expands again asking you whom (in CRM) you would like to have financial transactions with (Figure 6-16). Select *Accounts & their Contacts,* so Finance Suite apps features get enabled for both *Accounts* and *Contacts*.

Figure 6-16. *Indicating which CRM modules to work with financial transactions*

5. Click *Save* to finish the integration. Details of the integration will be shown (Figure 6-17). As long as the integration is active *Accounts* and their *Contacts, Vendors,* and *Products* information will be synced between CRM and enable Finance Suite apps.

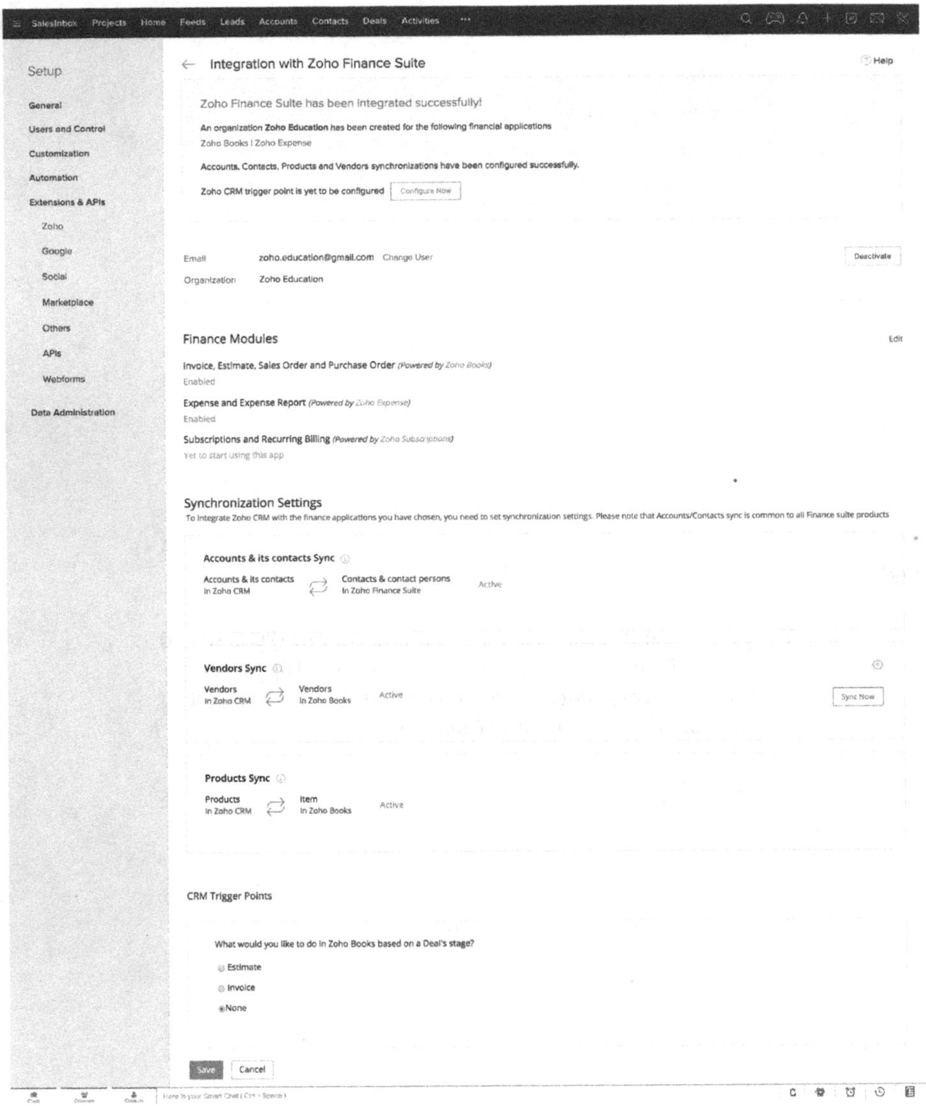

Figure 6-17. *Integrations details after a succesful connection between CRM and Finance Suite*

6. Hover the mouse curse over *Accounts & its contacts Sync* box (Figure 6-18). Then click on the settings icon (gear) to configure the sync.

Figure 6-18. Changing sync settings

7. In the sync settings page (Figure 6-19), review syncing modules, overwrite rules, and field-mappings between CRM and Finance Suite. For now, leave the values untouched and go back to the integration summary page.

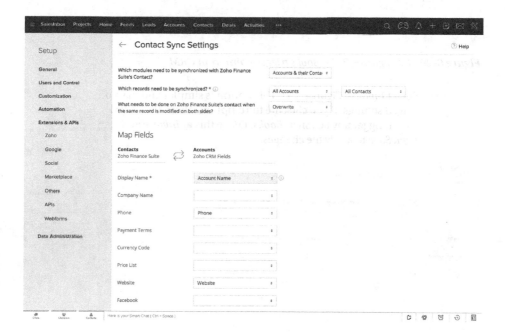

Figure 6-19. Sync settings page

8. In the integration page, scroll down to *CRM Trigger Points*. Here you can tell Zoho Books (the accounting app in the Finance Suite) what to do depending on the stage a CRM deal is in.

9. Click on Estimate (Figure 6-20) to review the available options. For instance, you can set up Zoho Books to create an estimate automatically when a deal is in the "Quote/Proposal" stage.

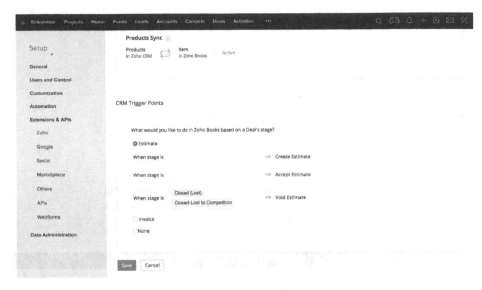

Figure 6-20. *Configuring Zoho Books trigger point from CRM*

10. Select *Invoice* (Figure 6-21). This option is simpler and has no staged settings. If you click the third option, *None*, then CRM won't trigger any action in *Books*. Leave this at *Invoice* and click *Save* to apply the changes.

Figure 6-21. *Setting a new invoice be created (or voided) in Zoho Books when a Deal stage is set to won (or lost)*

You can always come back and fine-tune the sync settings between CRM and the Finance Suite.

───

■ **Reference**   If you get stuck somewhere, feel free to refer to the official documentation at https://www.zoho.com/crm/help/zoho-finance-suite/.

───

Integrating with Zoho Creator

Zoho Creator is a powerful and easy-to-use business application creation platform. You can create simple or complex applications on the cloud: something as simple as a contact manager, a mini CRM, a complete real estate management system, or virtually any app that deals with business process and data.

Zoho CRM is quite customizable. Armed with features such as automation workflows, custom modules, and webforms, it can meet the requirements of most businesses. But as your business grows, your business requirements grow more complex as well.

In such a case, you can create customized apps with Zoho Creator and integrate them to be accessed from within the CRM. Creator apps also exchange data with CRM, meaning each can use information from the other one.

Also, you might be already using Zoho Creator and now you want to connect one or more Creator apps to CRM to extend its capabilities.

In a real-life example, a few years ago I had a client who had a team of telemarketers working for his company. These telemarketers, would open CRM, call leads and read through a sales script to pursue the person on the phone to buy their products. The sales script needed to be "smart" meaning it should have adapted itself to a person's feedback, showing only questions that were in line with the answers to the previous question. There should also be a way for the telemarketers to take note while on the phone.

After evaluating the requirements and considering available resources, constraints, and user experience factors, I decided to make Creator app and embed it into CRM. It worked perfectly and the client was very happy. Implementing a similar solution purely in CRM would have proved impossible. Creator, with minimal development work, improved the process dramatically.

■ **Shameless promotion**   In parallel to this book, I have written another one exclusively about Zoho Creator called *Zoho Creator: Build Cloud-Based Business Applications from the Ground Up* (Apress, 2017). I encourage you to read it and learn more about Zoho Creator if you are serious about creating high-quality cloud-based apps for SMEs with no or little programming background and minimal time and effort.

All said, you should make sure you are not reinventing the wheel and what you are trying to accomplish in Zoho Creator is not possible or is much harder to accomplish with CRM alone.

To enable Zoho Creator integration with Zoho CRM, follow these steps:

1. Open *Setup* ➤ *Extensions & APIs* ➤ *Zoho* ➤ *Build Custom App (Powered by Zoho Creator)*.

2. In the *Build Custom Apps* page (Figure 6-22), click on the *Enable Custom Apps* button.

Figure 6-22. *Enabling Zoho Creator integration*

A success message will appear indicating the integration was complete (Figure 6-23).

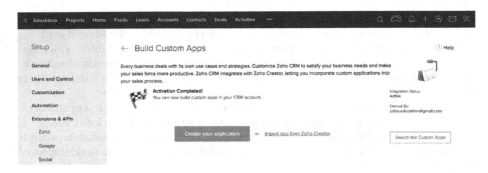

Figure 6-23. *Integration was successful*

Here, there are two options to choose from:

- to create a new Creator application, or
- to import an exiting one from Creator.

Clicking on the *Import from Zoho Creator* link will open the *Import App* dialog box, listing existing apps in your CRM account (Figure 6-24).

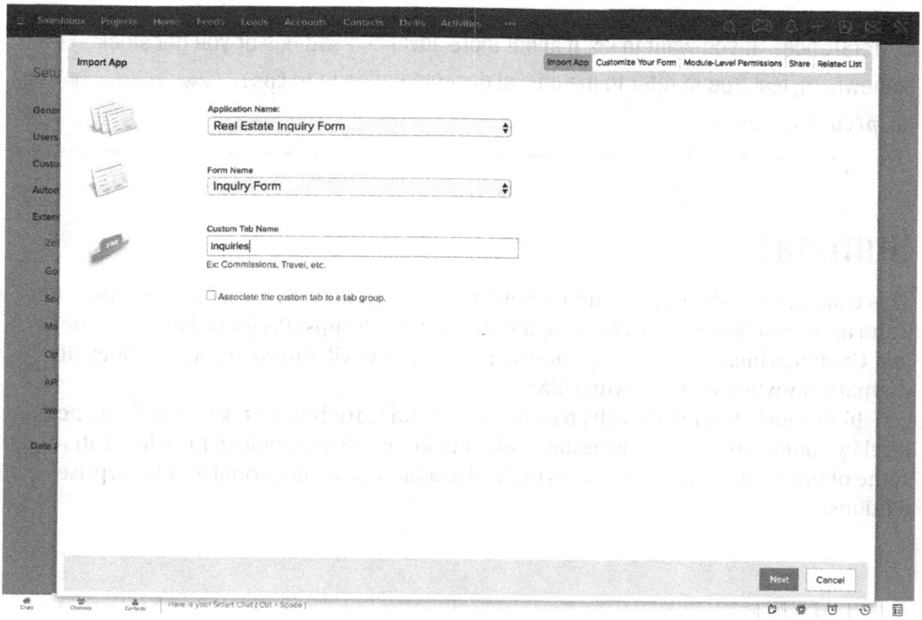

Figure 6-24. Importing an existing Creator app to CRM

On the other hand, clicking on the *Create Your Application* button will open the *Create Custom App* dialog box (Figure 6-25) where you can build a Creator app from scratch and then import it into CRM.

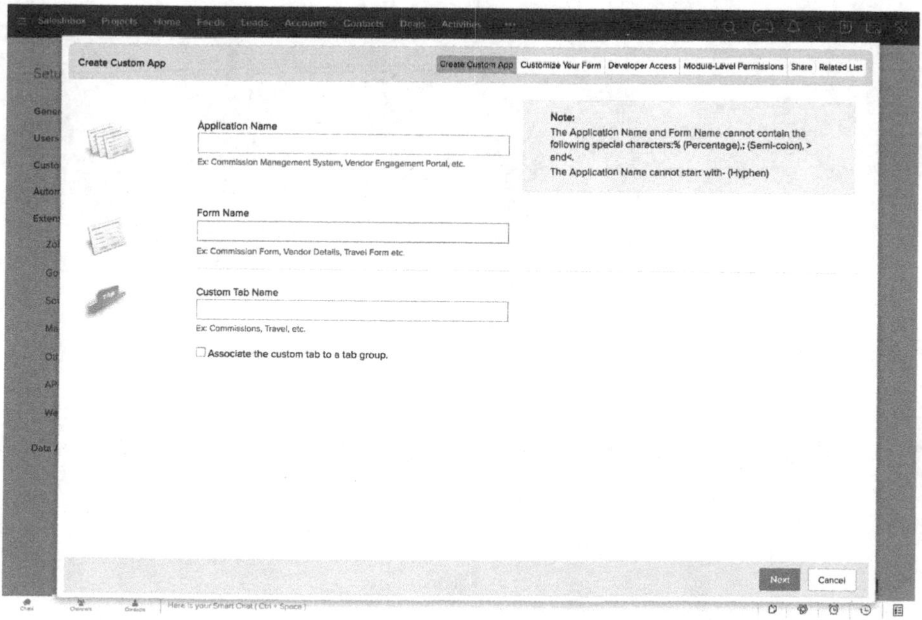

Figure 6-25. Creating a new Creator app from within CRM

■ **Reference**   If you want to learn about more advanced settings or you get stuck somewhere, feel free to refer to the official documentation at `https://www.zoho.com/crm/help/custom-apps/`.

Summary

This chapter was all about extending Zoho CRM capabilities by integrating it with other Zoho apps. You learned how to integrate some of these apps: Projects, Finance Suite, and Creator, which based on experience, I can say that will improve your productivity dramatically when coupled with CRM.

In the next chapter, we will go even further and learn how to take CRM to the next level by connecting it to the external world, but before that we will go into detail about some of the most advanced features of CRM available in Professional and Enterprise editions.

CHAPTER 7

■ ■ ■

Taking CRM and Your Business to the Next Level

So far in this book, we have covered all the essential features and tools available to you to run a more effective and more efficient sales and marketing operation in your organization using Zoho CRM. You should be able to confidently set up CRM based on your business requirements and provide your sales and marketing with a robust tool that helps them in their day-to-day work.

But CRM can do much more for you. In the previous chapter, you saw how CRM can work with other Zoho tools and extend its capabilities on different fronts.

The next step in unleashing the power of CRM is to let it automate key business processes, from sending simple notifications, to running complex workflows.

In this chapter, we will go through some of the more advanced features of Zoho CRM that are available in the Professional and Enterprise editions. Based on my personal experience with clients and colleagues, these two editions are the most popular because of the powerful host of features they offer and their (unbeatable) value for the money.

■ **Reference**   You can compare all editions of Zoho CRM and find the one most suitable for your requirements at https://www.zoho.com/crm/comparison.html.

Let's start with the most important topic, security, which must always be on top of your priority list, and not only for CRM, but for every single software, app, or online service that you are planning on using to store your personal or business information.

Security Management

In Chapter 3, you learned how to create users in CRM. However, when it comes to managing users and your organizational data in terms of who can access what, CRM offers a number of key features to help you control access to information down to individual records.

© Ali Shabdar 2017
A. Shabdar, *Mastering Zoho CRM*, DOI 10.1007/978-1-4842-2904-0_7

Zoho CRM offers security management in four different ways:

- **Users**: Each represents an employee of the organization;

- **Roles**: Such as *Manager*, which resemble the organizational hierarchy and allow the controlling of data sharing in CRM;

- **Profiles**: Such as *Standard*, which allow setting permissions to access features and tools at module, submodule, and field levels; and

- **Groups**: Such as *Sales*, which allow giving access to data to users with similar job profiles.

The very first CRM user is the one who created the Zoho CRM account in the first place. She or he automatically becomes the *Super Admin*, having full access to all the features and information in the CRM.

You (the Super Admin) must protect this user's id and password with your life. The person in your organization who holds the Super Admin account must be well versed in CRM and also have the highest clearance to access data, because nothing is hidden from the mighty Super Admin.

That's why in CRM, Super Admin's profile is set to *CEO*. Although they may not be the real CEO in the organization, they are the equivalent of a CEO in the CRM world.

When deciding about allocating different access levels to different parts of the organizational information in the CRM, look at your current processes. For example, if in you company only the senior management and above can see the financial state of the sales pipeline, then in the CRM, all pipeline-related views, reports, and dashboards that contain financial information, must be hidden from the any user that ranks lower than Director (or the role you define for your company).

Managing Users

As an admin (system administrator) you can create and delete users. You can also modify their information and reset their password.

As a refresher, let's have a quick look at the Users page by opening the CRM *Setup* page and clicking *Users* under *Users and Control*. The *Users* page will open (Figure 7-1).

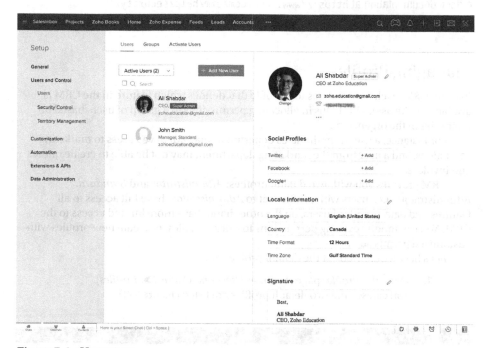

Figure 7-1. *Users page*

By default, your own user is selected in the users list. You can review and modify your role, organization information, signature, salutation, etc. You have access to the same for all other users too.

Clicking on Add New User will let you create more users. Notice that you may need to purchase more users if you have exhausted your available quota. When you create a new user in CRM, CRM allocates a profile (*Standard*, by default) and a role (*Manager*, by default) to that user. You will learn in the upcoming sections how to add more roles and profiles that match your business practice.

You can also deactivate other users to suspend their access to CRM temporarily without deleting them and possibly losing important information.

An important rule of thumb is to start giving the minimum possible access to information to each role and then give more access if necessary. The default *Standard* profile is not suitable for this purpose. Make sure you create a base profile (e.g., "Staff") defined in the CRM that has the bare-minimum access level and assign all users whom you are not yet sure how much access you need to give them to that role. We will cover this in a bit.

■ **Reference**   To learn more about CRM's security management features, refer to the official documentation at https://www.zoho.com/crm/help/security/.

Managing Profiles

In Zoho CRM, each user belongs to a profile that defines which feature in the CRM is available to the user. This helps in allocating permissions to a group of users based on their roles in the organization.

For instance, a user from the sales department may not have access to marketing campaigns, and a user from the marketing department may not be able to create quotes and invoices.

CRM provides you with two default profiles: *Administrator* and *Standard*. Administrators (i.e., users with profiles set to *Administrator*) have full access to all features and data. Standard users, on the other hand, have more limited access to the CRM. You can modify existing permissions for these profiles, or create new profiles with customized permissions.

Let's have a quick look at the default profiles first:

1.   Open the *Profiles* page (*Setup* ➤ *Users and Control* ➤ *Profiles*).
You can see the two default profiles are listed (Figure 7-2).

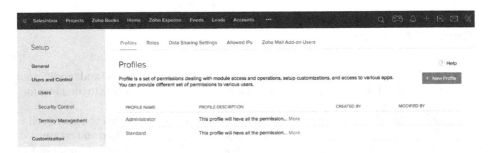

Figure 7-2. *Profiles page*

2. Click on the *Administrator* profile in the list. The profile details with all the permissions will be displayed (Figure 7-3).

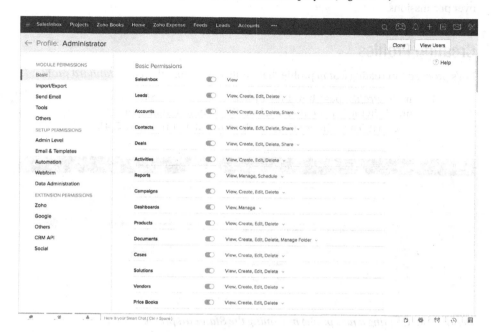

Figure 7-3. *Administrator profile page*

3. Review the list of permissions. You can see that on/off switches for some of the permissions are enabled and some are not. You can disable access to certain modules for administrators, but essential administrative permissions, such as import and export, and user management remain on at all times. Go back to the list of profiles by clicking on the back arrow icon on the top left of the screen.

4. Now, open the *Standard* profile. Quite similar to the Administrator page, you can see the permissions listed – some of which are changeable and some are not.

Standard profile can't manage users (add, edit, remove) or perform data migration and a couple of other sensitive operations. Otherwise it is quite similar to *Administrator* profile.

■ **Note**   As a best practice, it is recommended to disable or hide any module, submodule, field, or feature that is not used in your organization to avoid clutter and confusion. So, if in your organization, you don't use one or some of the default CRM modules, for example, Sales Orders, you can disable them in the profiles for all profiles. This way no one will see the unnecessary modules. You can always bring them back by enabling disabled modules in the profiles.

Since switching many permissions on or off are disabled for the default profiles, we should leave these two alone and instead create our own profiles to have more control over permissions.

Creating Profiles

Let's proceed by creating a *Staff* profile that limits users more than the *Standard* profile:

1. In the *Profiles* page hover the mouse cursor on the *Standard* profile in the list and then click on the ... button that appears next to it. Then choose *Clone* in the context menu (Figure 7-4).

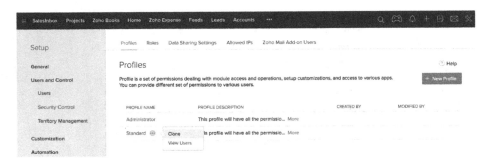

Figure 7-4. *Creating a new profile by cloning the Standard profile*

2. Fill in the *Create new profile* form as you see in Figure 7-5. Then click *Create* to proceed.

Figure 7-5. *Creating a new profile by cloning the Standard profile*

3. In the profile details page, you can see that more permission switches are enabled and you have more control over them compared to *Standard* profile. Continue by turning the following permissions off:

   a. *Delete* and *Share* (if available) permissions for all modules as you see in Figure 7-6.

Figure 7-6. *Disabling Delete and Share permissions for all modules*

    b.   Forecast module

    c.   Import Organization Record

    d.   Export

    e.   Mass Email

    f.   Delete Email

    g.   Mass Update

    h.   Change Owner

    i.   Mass Transfer

    j.   Mass Convert

    k.   Sheet View

    l.   Setup Permissions (will disable some other permissions).

   4.   Click the back arrow icon on the top left of the screen to return to the profiles list.

The newly created profile, *Staff*, is a good starting point for all users who don't need advanced permissions. If you see in the future that users in this profile need more, or less permissions, you can come back and turn a specific permission on or off for them with immediate effect across the CRM.

Unlike default profiles, you can delete custom profiles by clicking on the corresponding ... button and selecting *Delete* in the context menu. You will be asked to transfer any user that is currently under that profile to another profile. Be careful here as you may inadvertently give extra (or less) permissions by transferring users to another profile.

Managing Roles

Zoho CRM allows you to simulate your organizational hierarchy using Roles. Roles in CRM are about data access. Users at a higher level (e.g., senior management) can access all the records of the users at a lower level. For instance, a Sales Manager can access all the information entered (and owned) by sales representatives.

By default, there are two roles in the CRM: *CEO* and *Manager*. Obviously, users with a *CEO* role (yes, there can be more than one CEO in the CRM world) have access to all the information stored in the CRM. *Managers*, on the other hand, can only view or edit their subordinates' records if they have the *Read* or *Edit* permissions. You can define data sharing rules in Zoho CRM to allow roles, such as peers, who do not see certain information by default, to access specific information. To make these assertions make more sense, let's continue by creating a number of new roles and then look at data sharing.

Creating Roles

To create a new role, follow these steps:

1. In the CRM, open the *Security Control* page (*Setup* ➤ *Users and Control* ➤ *Security Control*.

2. Click *Roles* on the top tab bar. *Roles* page will open showing the default roles in a hierarchical manner (Figure 7-7).

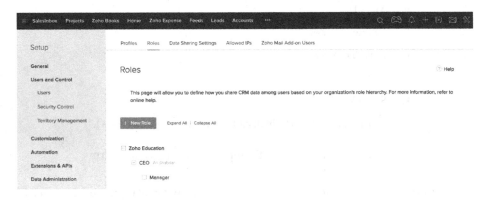

Figure 7-7. *Roles page*

3. Click on the New Role button. In the New Role form, populate the form as you see in Figure 7-8 to create a new Director role.

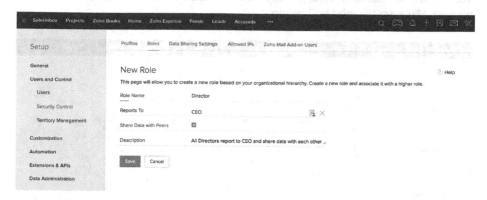

Figure 7-8. *Creating new "Director" role*

    a. To select a role for *Reports To* field, click the *Role Name Lookup* icon next to it and then select *CEO* in the *Roles List* dialog box.

    b. Click *Save* when you are done.

4. The details of the newly created role will be shown (Figure 7-9). You can edit the role if needed, or delete it if you change your mind. For now, simply click on *Go to Roles* List.

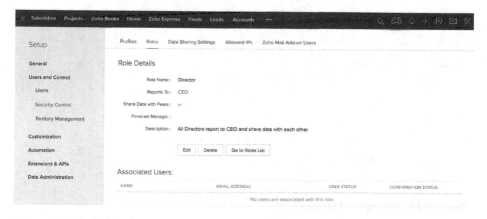

Figure 7-9. *Role detail page showing the details of the Director role*

In the *Roles* page, hovering on the Director role, you can see a context bar appearing allowing you to add subordinates to this role, as well as to edit or delete it (Figure 7-10). You can also see that both *Manager* and *Director* roles are listed under the *CEO*; however, we want Managers to report to Directors.

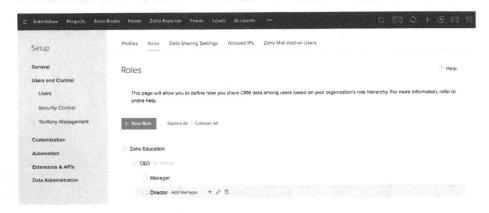

Figure 7-10. *Roles hierarchy and role context bar*

So, instead of adding a new role under Director, we can move the existing Manager role under Director.

To do so, hover the mouse cursor on the *Manager* role and click the pencil icon to edit the role.

Then in the Edit Role page (Figure 7-11), change *Reports To* to Director and click *Save* to apply the changes.

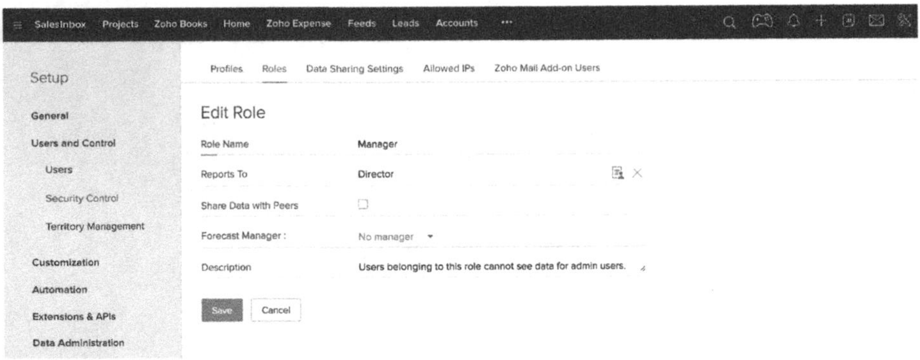

Figure 7-11. *Editing the Manager role*

Now if you go back to the *Roles* page (Figure 7-12), you should see the role *Manager* is placed under the *Director*, and it, under the *CEO*.

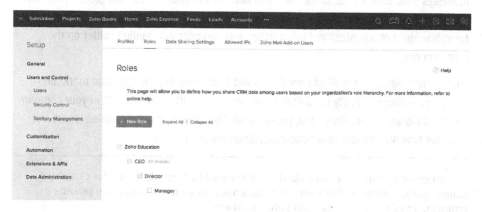

Figure 7-12. *Updated organizational hierarchy*

EXERCISE

Add more roles matching the organizational chart of your company and create the proper hierarchy for them in the CRM. Indicate which roles can share data among peers.

Managing Data Sharing

You learned earlier that in Zoho CRM, the default setting is only the record (any piece of information, such as a lead, contact, etc.) owner and their manager. Users in other roles can see information that they or their subordinates have not created.

Data sharing rules in CRM will help you override the default settings and provide access to other roles and groups according to your business requirements.

For instance, if in your company, the Digital Marketing Manager needs to have read-only access to everyone's Campaigns information, you can enable this by defining a specific data sharing rule. Then users with that role can see all campaign records in the system.

■ **Note** Don't get overgenerous and give extra access to data to people who don't need it. Always keep data access to the minimum number of people, roles, and groups possible. This way, you have better control over information leakage, make less people accountable for safekeeping of organizational information, and minimize information clutter on the receiving end.

For instance, although the VP of Operation could technically see all sales and marketing information, does she really need that many records to clutter her view? If, in your company, she needs to see sales information, provide a limited, clear, and concise sales report and save her time and yourself less headaches down the road.

In general, you can set data sharing rules for all CRM modules, such as Leads, Contacts, etc., except for Forecasts. Attachments, notes, emails, and other records connected to a record are also accessible to others.

There are three types of access levels in Zoho CRM:

- **Private:** Access is limited to the record owner and their superior,

- **Public Read only:** Other users can only view records that are made public without the ability to modify and delete them, and

- **Public Read/Write/Delete:** Other users have full access over records that are made public.

Managing Default Permissions

Suppose we need to make vendor and product information publicly available to all users, so no matter who created a vendor, or a product, everyone can access their information.

To change default data sharing permissions for *Vendors* and *Products*, follow these steps:

1. Open *Data Sharing Setting* page via *Setup* ➤ *Users & Control* ➤ *Security Control* ➤ *Data Sharing Settings*. All modules will be listed with their current access permissions (Figure 7-13).

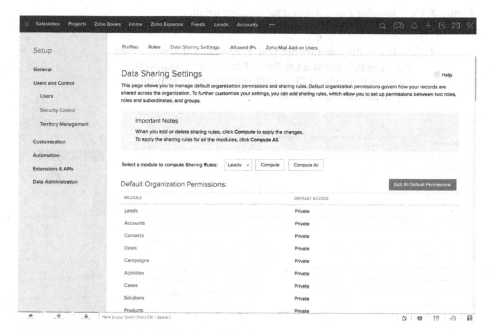

Figure 7-13. *Data Sharing Settings page*

2. Find Products in the modules list and click on it. In the *Edit Default Organization Permission* dialog box, select *Public Read Only* in the drop-down list for *Default Access* (Figure 7-14). Click *Save* to continue.

Figure 7-14. *Changing Deafult Access for Products module*

3. Repeat step 2 (above) for the *Vendors* module (Figure 7-15).

Figure 7-15. *Changing Deafult Access for Vendors module*

4. Notice in the modules list, both *Products* and *Vendors* have their *Default Access* set to *Public Read Only*. To apply the changes throughout CRM, click the *Compute All* button on top of the list (Figure 7-16).

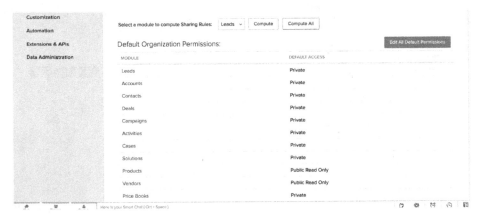

Figure 7-16. *Default Access changed for Products and Vendors modules*

Creating Data Sharing Rules

There are many scenarios where changing default permissions at module level (see previous section) are just what you need. However, you may want to give more controlled access to some users beyond a mere public read/write/delete permission.

Fortunately, Zoho CRM allows you to define data sharing rules at role and group level.

For instance, suppose your CEO receives leads in her meetings, which her Executive Assistant (who has access to CEO's CRM account) enters in the CRM. Now, we cannot rely on the CEO and her super busy schedule to respond to leads in a timely fashion, so we need the Sales Director to see these leads and act upon them accordingly. This way, the lead owner remains to be the CEO and managing the lead will be the Sales Director's job.

Follow these steps to give the Director role access to see the CEO's leads:

1.   Open *Data Sharing Setting* page via *Setup* ➤ *Users & Control* ➤ *Security Control* ➤ *Data Sharing Setting.*

2.   Scroll down the page until you see Sharing Rules section (Figure 7-17).

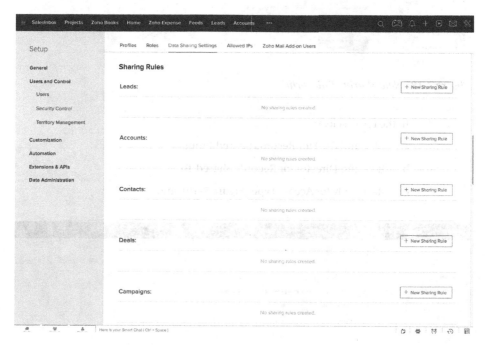

Figure 7-17. *Sharing Rules section in Data Sharing Settings page*

3. Click on the *New Sharing Rule* button in front of the *Leads* subsection. The *New Sharing Rule* form will open (Figure 7-18).

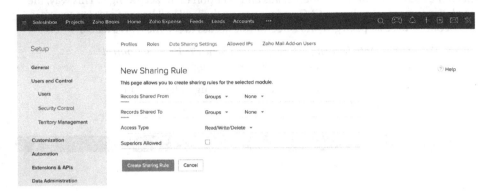

Figure 7-18. *New Sharing Rule form*

4. In the form, select:

    a. Role and CEO for Records Shared From,

    b. Role and Director for Records Shared To,

    c. Read Only for Access Type (Figure 7-19), and

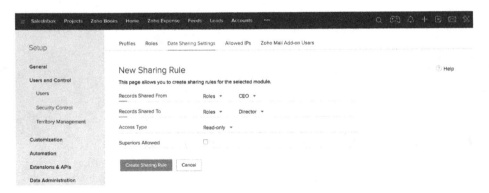

Figure 7-19. *Sharing Rule form populated with a new rule*

    d. Click Create Sharing Rule to add the rule.

You can see the new rule listed under *Sharing Rules* ➤ *Leads* (Figure 7-20). You can edit or delete this rule and the changes to access permissions will take effect immediately.

Figure 7-20. *New sharing rule is listed under Leads*

■ **Note**   In the above example we gave access to the CEO's leads to the Director role. This means all users at Director level (e.g., Sales, Marketing, Operations, etc.) can see the CEO's leads. If you want to give the Sales Director only access to these leads, you need to first create a new Sales Director role, assign the corresponding user to this role, and then create the data sharing rule.

Sharing

There is yet another deeper level of sharing data in Zoho CRM and that is Record-Level Sharing. Record-level sharing allows you (or any CRM user) to share only a specific set of records with specific users. You can share as many records as you want and from any module (except Forecasts) that you want.

For instance, if you want to share the 25 leads you collected in an exhibition you and your colleague Daenerys attended together last week, you can easily select those leads and share them with her.

FURTHER READING

Share a number of leads and a contact with another user using record-level sharing. Give only read access to leads. For the contact, give read/write access to the contact and read access to related deals.

Consult the official documentation if you get stuck: `https://www.zoho.com/crm/help/security/record-level-sharing.html`.

Managing Groups

Sometimes you need to grant access to specific data in Zoho CRM to a group of users who are not in the same role (level), reporting hierarchy, or department. In such case, roles alone will not help you. You will need to utilize groups.

For instance, as a part of an internal audit project, you may need to give temporary access to all invoices in the CRM to all Directors, Finance Managers, and two employees from the Finance department.

CRM Groups let you put users, roles (and subordinates), and other groups (and subgroups) into a single group and then create data sharing rules for that group.

Let's create a group and share all Accounts information with them:

1. Open Groups page from *Setup* ➤ *Users & Control* ➤ *Users* ➤ *Groups*. There are no groups by default (Figure 7-21).

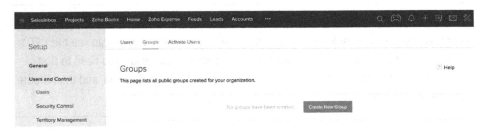

Figure 7-21. *Groups page*

2. Click on the *Create Group* button. The *New Group* form will open (Figure 7-22).

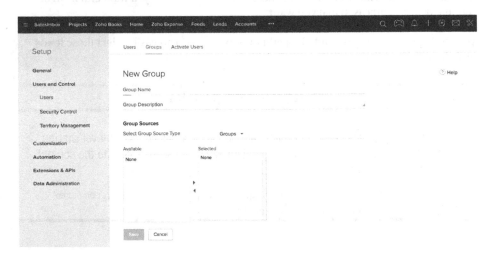

Figure 7-22. *Creating a new group*

3. Fill in the form as you see in Figure 7-23:

   a. Give new group a name and a description.

   b. Under *Group Sources*, select *Roles* for *Select Group Source Type*.

   c. You can see the existing CRM roles get listed under *Available* pick list. Select the *Director* role and click the *Add* button (little right arrow) to add it to the *Selected* pick list on the right side.

   d. We need to add a user to the group as well. Under *Group Sources*, select *Users* for *Select Group Source Type*.

   e. CRM users get listed under *Available* pick list. Select a user and click the *Add* button to add it to the *Selected* pick list on the right side.

   f. Click *Save* to create the new group.

Figure 7-23. *Populating the new group form*

4. You will be redirected to the group details page where you can see users, roles, roles and subordinates, and other groups associated with the newly created group (Figure 7-24).

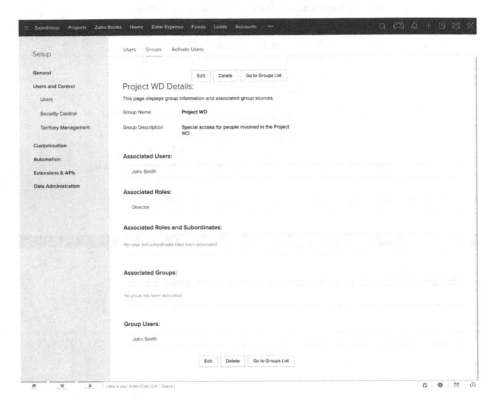

Figure 7-24. *Group details page*

Automating Business Processes

When the first computers were built in the 1960s, humanity, as a naturally intelligent and lazy species, got one step closer to its dream of automating mundane tasks by machines to save our most precious asset, time.

Fast forward to today. Our electronic friends (or frenemies in the near future) have automated most of our lives giving us enough time to do more important things, such as taking millions of pictures of ourselves and our food and sharing the glory with the world to enjoy.

Zoho CRM, too, provides powerful features that allow users to automate repeated tasks away from delays and human error. Autoresponders, alerts and notifications, data sharing rules, territory management, and a few other essential features make it easier to rely on CRM to perform a number of basic tasks and help us stay productive.

There are also more advanced features, such as workflows, assignment rules, website integrations, scoring rules, and the recent Blueprint that focus on automating and streamlining business processes of an organization.

■ **Note** We will review some of the business process automation tools and features of Zoho CRM in this chapter. You can learn more about other existing and new features in the official documentation at `https://www.zoho.com/crm/help/automation/`.

Workflow Automation

Workflows are series of activities or processes that are performed in a specific sequence to accomplish a task. A workflow can be manual, partially, or fully automated. Workflows often contain a set of rules and criteria in them.

For instance, here is a simple customer service workflow:

- Trigger: when a deal is finalized.
- Activities:
    - send a reminder to the sales person to send the client a thank you email and a feedback form, and
    - send a notification to the sales manager to review the sales report.

This workflow can be automated even further to send the thank you note and the feedback form automatically without the interference of the salesperson in charge, and also email the sales report to the sales manager directly.

A workflow could also trigger another workflow. In the example above, when a feedback form is sent to the client, upon submission of the form, another workflow can be triggered that notifies both the salesperson and the manager, as well as the marketing team.

By looking at the simple workflow, you can guess how much manual work you can ask CRM to do for you automatically. This will save your team a ton of time, minimizes errors and omissions, and ensures that business processes are followed to the dot.

To help you get the most out of workflows in Zoho CRM, you can use a mix of the following tools:

- **Workflow Rules:** which are triggered when specific criteria are met, for example when a deal is finalized;

- **Workflow Alerts:** which send email notifications when specific workflow rules are triggered, for example, a thank you email;

- **Workflow Tasks:** which assign tasks to users when specific workflow rules are triggered, for example, a report submission task;

- **Workflow Field Updates:** which change the value of specific fields when workflow rules are triggered, for example, setting the value of the *Next Step* for a won *Deal* to "*Receive Client Feedback*";

- **Webhooks:** which send web notifications (i.e., HTTP requests) to third-party applications when an event is triggered in the CRM, for example, sending an external accounting system financial information when an invoice is issued in the CRM; and

- **Custom Functions:** which allow you to write scripts (small programs intended to do a limited set of tasks) using Zoho's proprietary scripting language, Deluge, to communicate with external apps and services and make changes in Zoho CRM, for example, receive inventory data every night from a remote server and update CRM inventory automatically.

■ **Reference**   Deluge (stands for the mouthful Data Enriched Language for the Universal Grid Environment) is Zoho's proprietary scripting language that allows you to write complex scripts in Zoho CRM and Zoho Creator and extend their capabilities dramatically. If you are familiar with programming and planning to impressive stuff in CRM, indulge yourself with the official Deluge documentation: `https://www.zoho.com/creator/help/script`.

Creating Workflow Rules

To learn more about workflow automation let's start by creating a workflow rule:

1. Open *Workflow Rules* page via *Settings* ➤ *Setup* ➤ *Automation* ➤ *Workflow Rules*. There is a demo workflow rule called *Big Deal Rule* already in the list of rules (Figure 7-25). Ignore this one for now and study it later.

Figure 7-25. *Workflow Rules page*

2.   Click on the *Create Rule* button. *Create Rule* dialog box will appear (Figure 7-26).

Figure 7-26. *Creating a new workflow rule*

3.   In the *Create Rule* dialog box, select *Deals* for *Module*, then type in a *Rule Name* and a *Description* as you see in Figure 7-27. Click *Save* to continue.

Figure 7-27. *Create Rule dialog box populated*

4.   A new page will open showing a visual representation of the workflow rule (Figure 7-28). Continue by setting "when" the workflow has to trigger.

Figure 7-28. *Workflow visual designer*

5. Select *On a record action* under the question *When do you want to execute this rule?* A list of possible actions will appear (Figure 7-29).

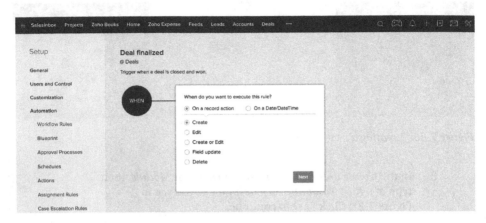

Figure 7-29. *Choosing the workflow to trigger on a specific record event*

6. Select *Field update* for an action and then select the *Stage* from the first drop-down that lists the fields of the Deals module (Figure 7-30). Click *Next* to continue.

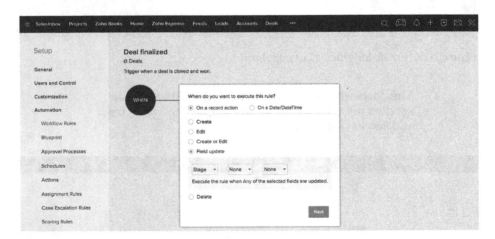

Figure 7-30. *Choosing the workflow to trigger when a deal's Stage field gets updated*

7. In the next step, you need to know which records will be affected by the workflow. Leave the selections as you see in Figure 7-31.

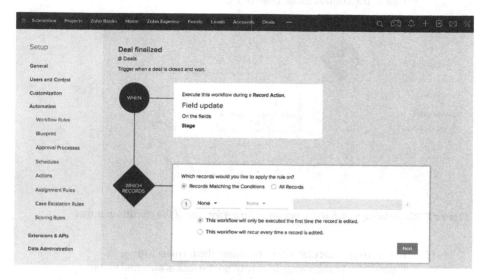

Figure 7-31. *Narrowing down subject records to a specific set*

8. For the first condition (you can add more if you like), select *Stage*, *is*, and *Closed (Won)* (Figure 7-32). This indicates that the workflow runs only when a deal stage is won and finalized. Click *Next* to continue.

Figure 7-32. *Setting the workflow to run only on deals, which stage is Closed (won)*

9. Next, you will be setting which actions the workflow will perform, starting with creating and assigning a task for the deal owner. Click on the *Instant Action* box and then select *Task* in the context menu (Figure 7-33).

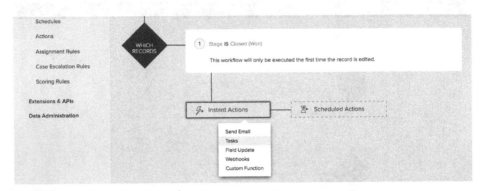

Figure 7-33. *Adding a task as an action to be performed if the condition is met*

10. In the *Assign Task* dialog box, populate the form as you see in Figure 7-34. Leave Assign To empty, so the task is assigned to the deal owner. Then click *Save and Associate* when you are done.

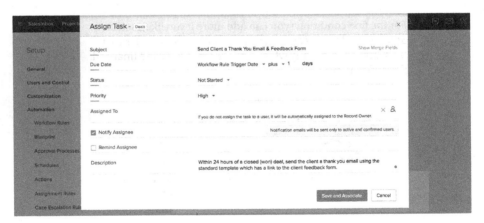

Figure 7-34. *Creating a task for the record (deal) owner*

11. Back in the workflow designer, add another action and this time select *Send Mail* (Figure 7-35). We will need to inform the deal owner's manager about winning the deal.

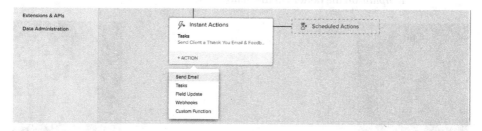

Figure 7-35. *Adding a new action to the workflow*

12. In the *Send Alert* dialog box (Figure 7-36), click *New Alert*.

Figure 7-36. *Send Alert dialog box*

13. In the *Send Alert* dialog box, give the alert a name and select *Deal Owner's Manager* in the recipients as shown in Figure 7-37. You can select more recipients from other modules and also type in additional email addresses if you like.

Figure 7-37. *Setting up the email alert*

203

14. Click *Select Template* button and in the template selector dialog box (Figure 7-38), choose one of the existing templates, or create a new one for this workflow by clicking *Create Template* on the bottom of the dialog box.

Figure 7-38. *Email (alert) template selector dialog box*

15. Once you select a template, you will be back to the *Send Alert* dialog box. Review the entries and click *Save* and Associate.

16. We are done. The final workflow is show in the visual designer (Figure 7-39). Click *Save* to create the workflow rule.

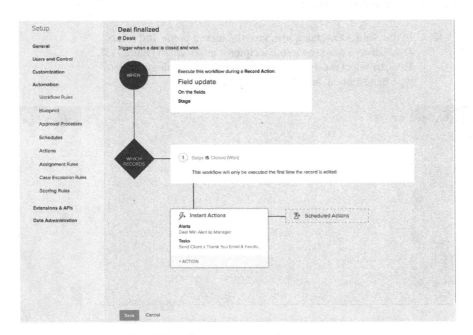

Figure 7-39. *Finished workflow deisgn waiting to be stored*

You will be redirected to the *Workflow Rules* page (Figure 7-40). The newly created workflow is listed here and is active (the green switch on the right side is on). You can always come back to this page to modify, deactivate, or permanently delete workflow rules.

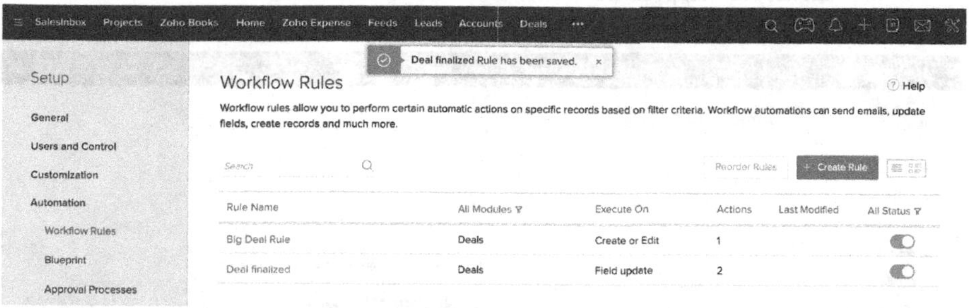

Figure 7-40. *Workflow rules page with new workflow listed and active*

Make sure you test your workflows and check whether every single step works as intended. For our sample workflow here, you would be moving a (dummy) deal to the *Closed (Won)* stage and then check if a task was created and assigned to the deal owner, and an email was sent to the deal owner's manager announcing a win.

You can add schedule workflows, create multiple workflows that work in parallel, and have some of these workflows trigger other workflows. I will leave further exploration to your imagination and, of course, your business requirements.

Approvals Automation

In almost any business beyond a one-person operation, obtaining approvals for certain tasks is the norm. Approvals and sign-offs help managing the junior personnel better and double-check when a potentially sensitive step is about to be taken. It also clarifies and enforces accountability and chain of command in an organization.

For instance, giving an extra discount to a buyer, ordering a product more than the normal monthly quota, or even sending a quote to an opportunity may need approval (or sign-off) from one or more superiors.

In smaller companies, approval may be simply a verbal confirmation, or an email sent to managers; however, in the bigger organizations approvals are an important part of the business process and must be followed specifically so everyone keeps their jobs.

Zoho CRM provides an approval process to help you automate various approval processes in your organization.

Creating Approval Processes

Suppose, in your company, moving a deal to the *Quote* stage needs approval from the Sales Director. Instead of getting the sign-off manually (calling, emailing, etc.), setting up an approval process will automate this task and ensure that no deal enters the quote stage without written consent of the Sales Director.

Follow these steps to create the suitable approval process for the deals:

1. *Open Settings ➤ Setup ➤ Automation ➤ Approval Processes.*
   An empty *Approval Process* page will open (Figure 7-41). Click
   on the *New Approval Process* button to continue.

Figure 7-41. *Empty Approval processes page*

2. Populate the *New Approval Process* form as you see in
   Figure 7-42. This indicates that the approval process will
   trigger when a deal gets edited (changing *Stage* is considered
   an edit). Click *Add Rule to this process* to continue.

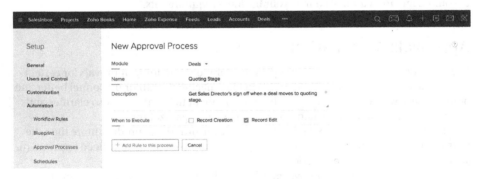

Figure 7-42. *Adding a new approval process*

3. In the next form, start by setting the *Rule Criteria* (Figure 7-43), which indicates which records are affected. *Select Stage, is,* and *Proposal/Price Quote* for the criteria.

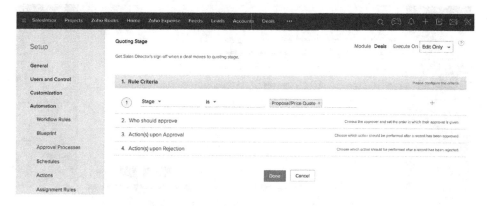

Figure 7-43. *Setting the rule criteria*

4. Then set who the approver(s) are. In our case, it is the *Director Role* (Figure 7-44). You can add more than one role or user as an approver.

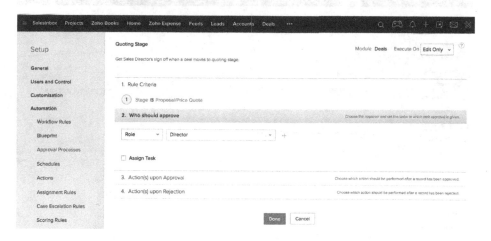

Figure 7-44. *Setting the approvers*

5. Check the *Assign Task* box and fill in the *Assign Task* dialog box (Figure 7-45) to create a task and a reminder for the approver to remember to approve the process in a timely fashion.

Figure 7-45. *Creating and assigning a new task for approver(s)*

6. Move on to section 3, *Action(s) upon Approval* (Figure 7-46). This is where you set what actually happens in the CRM when a process gets approved.

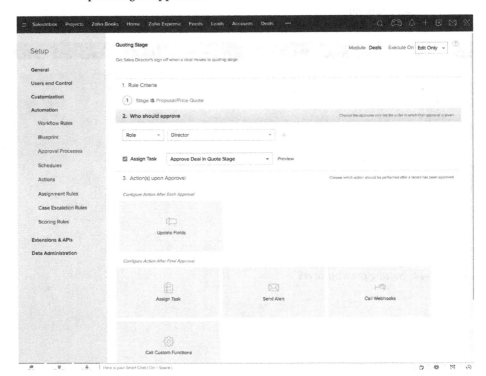

Figure 7-46. *Setting actions to be taken once a process is approved*

7. Click on the *Update Fields* gray box to set the action that happens for each approver. Since we have only one approver here, *Update Field* will happen once, but for scenarios with multiple approvers you should come up with a better alternative.

8. In the *Update Fields* dialog box (Figure 7-47), select *Next Step* in the field's drop-down. Then enter "*Send Quote – Approved.*" This will cause the *Next Step* field value to be updated with *Send Quote – Approved* as an indicator that the request is approved.

Figure 7-47. *Setting which fields will be updated as a result of an approval*

9. Click *Done* to close the *Update Fields* dialog box.

10. Next, you will configure actions that will happen only after everyone in the approving chain has approved the process. Click on *Assign Task*.

11. In the Assign Task dialog box (Figure 7-48), you can choose from a list of existing tasks, or create a new one. Click on the *New Task* button to proceed.

Figure 7-48. *Assigning a task to be assigned once the approval is obtained*

12. Populate the *Assign Task* dialog box similar to Figure 7-49 to create a task and a reminder to the record owner (person who owns the deal and seeks approval) to proceed with sending the client a quote. Click *Save and Associate* when you are done.

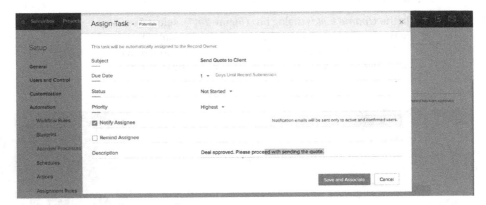

Figure 7-49. *Assigning a task to the deal owner*

13. Back in the rule page, you can see the two actions (Figure 7-50). Feel free to add more actions if necessary. Then move on to section 4.

Figure 7-50. *Actions upon approval are listed*

14. In section 4, *Action(s) upon Rejection* (Figure 7-51), you provision actions for when, for some reason, the approval request is rejected. Click on *Update Fields* to continue.

Figure 7-51. *List of possible actions to be executed if an approval request is rejected*

15. In the *Update Fields* dialog box (Figure 7-52), select Next Step in the field's drop-down list and type in *"Needs Further Review"* in the *Value*. Click *Done* to continue.

Figure 7-52. *Updating a field upon rejection of an approval*

16. Back in the rule page, you can see the *Update Fields* action is created for rejection (Figure 7-53). Click *Done* to proceed.

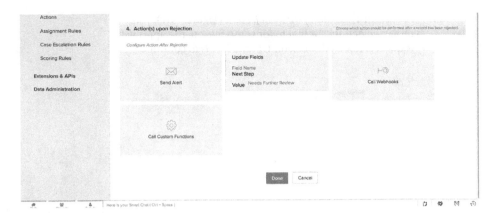

Figure 7-53. *The only action that will happen if the approval gets rejected*

17. You will be redirected to the approval process page with the one rule you just created showing in the page (Figure 7-54). You can still add more rules by clicking *Add Another Rule* and go through a similar process as just seen to add more rules. For now, just click on the *Save* button to create the approval process.

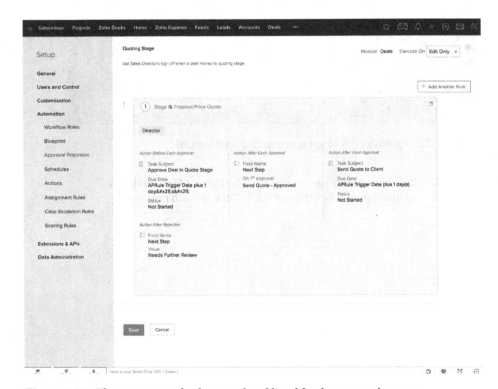

Figure 7-54. *The one approval rule created and listed for the approval process*

You will be redirected to the *Approval Process* List page (Figure 7-55). You can add more approval processes, as well as edit or delete the existing ones.

Figure 7-55. *List of all existing approval processes*

Note the green switch next to each approval process in the list. It allows you to deactivate and activate a process as needed.

Blueprint

There is no doubt that day-to-day business consists of a series of complex processes and subprocesses. There are main activities, such as sales, procurement, finance, and logistics, and then there is the business as a whole that needs to keep all units in check and push forward.

To ensure success in day-to-day operations and achieve strategic goals too, robust and efficient business processes must be designed and followed to the dot by all involved parties. Following policy and procedure is not easy nor is it exciting. Human beings are prone to error and sometimes they cut corners. It is even more severe in the case of a new workforce simply because they lack experience.

Training and having process maps handy definitely help, but what if there was a tool that could guide the employees through every step of a process? Fortunately, Zoho CRM just introduced the tool, Blueprint.

Blueprint lets you map the entire business process of your business (well, the ones that fit in the CRM capabilities) and have it facilitate process automation and validation, improve productivity and stop loopholes and missed steps from happening.

Creating a Blueprint Process

To learn a bit more about this exciting tool, we are going to create a simple process that guides users about the stages of contacting a lead.

Each lead has a *Lead Source* property (field), which by default is empty and could take one of these values:

- *Pre-Qualified,*
- *Not Contacted,*
- *Attempted to Contact,*
- *Contact in the Future,*

- *Contacted,*

- *Junk Lead,* and

- *Lost Lead.*

You may want to change these default states according to your needs; however, we will work with these in this scenario.

The idea is to instead of letting the user change *Lead Status* arbitrarily, enforce a process where a certain order is followed.

Follow these steps to define the supporting Blueprint process:

1. Open *Blueprint* page via *Settings* ➤ *Setup* ➤ *Automation* ➤ *Blueprint*. Then in the *Blueprint* page (Figure 7-56), click on the *Create Blueprint* button.

Figure 7-56. *Bluprint page*

2. Populate the fields in the *Create new Blueprint* dialog box as you see in Figure 7-57 and click *Next* when you are done:

   a. *Blueprint name*: "*Contacting Leads*"

   b. *Module*: *Leads*

   c. *Choose Layout*: *Standard*

   d. *Choose Field*: *Lead Status*

   e. *Criteria*: *Lead Owner, is, Logged in User*

Figure 7-57. *Creating a new Blueprint*

3. In the Blueprint visual designer (Figure 7-58), you can see the list of available states for the process, which is basically the list of statuses from *Lead Source* field. Drag *Not Contacted* from the list (left) to the designer (right) and drop it on the big circle in the middle.

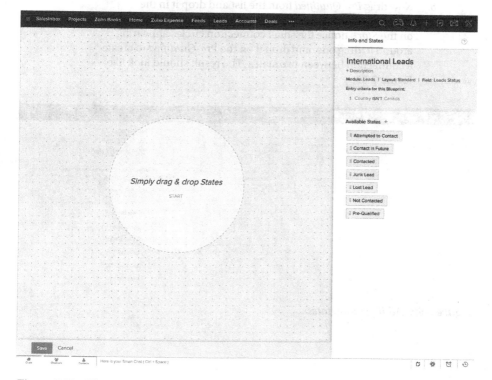

Figure 7-58. *Blueprint visual designer*

4. Blueprint automatically creates a small process with a *Start* point and connects it to a *Not Contacted* state (Figure 7-59). Each rectangle represents a stage in the process and the arrowed line is a connection showing the flow of the process.

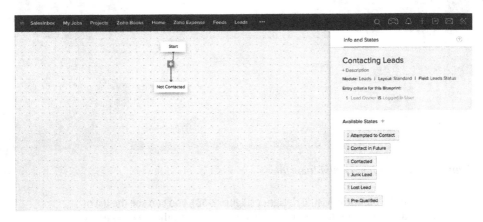

Figure 7-59. *Adding the first state in the process*

5. Now drag *Pre-Qualified* from the list and drop it in the designer adjacent to *Not Contacted*. Then hover the cursor on the *Start*, notice the small connection circles appearing around it, drag one, and drop it on the Pre-*Qualified* to create a connection between two states. The result should look like Figure 7-60.

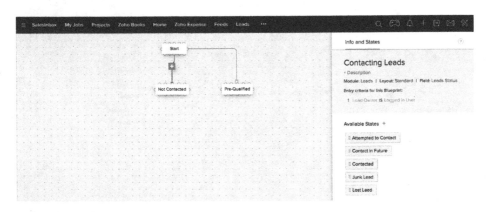

Figure 7-60. *Adding more states*

6.   Similarly, drag and drop other states and connect them as
      shown in Figure 7-61. You can actually read the process map
      and follow the logic. For instance, in real life, if a lead gets
      Pre-Qualified, the process end there, but if it is set to Not
      Contacted, you can still turn it into a *Contacted* or *Attempted
      to Contact*.

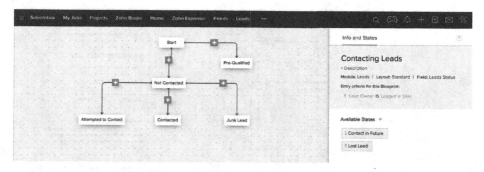

Figure 7-61. *Completing the process map*

7.   Next, we need to tell Blueprint what happens when the state
      changes. Using *Transitions* you can dictate the action that
      takes place between two states of the process. Click on the red
      plus button between *Start* and *Pre-Qualified*.

8.   Notice on the right sidebar a new tab shows up called
      Transitions (Figure 7-62). Type in "*Prequalify This Lead*" in
      the *Transition Name* and click *Save*. This transition will show
      up in a lead's details page as a button, so the user can simply
      click it to set the state. More on this in the next section.

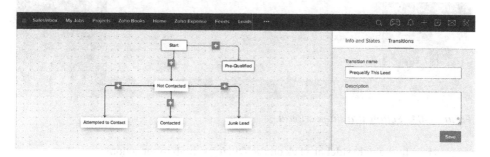

Figure 7-62. *Adding the first transition*

217

9. A green parallelogram representing the transition you just
    created will replace the red plus between the two states in
    the process map (Figure 7-63). Also the Transitions tab in the
    right side bar, will be divided into three subtabs for *Before*,
    During, and *After* the transition happens. Continue by clicking
    the *Add Criteria* link in the bottom of the *Before* subtab.

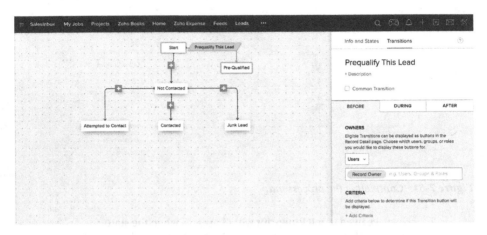

Figure 7-63. *Configuring the transition*

10. In the *Transition* criteria dialog box (Figure 7-64), select *Country*,
    is, and enter "*Canada*." This will tell the *Blueprint* to show a
    Pre-Qualify This *Lead* button in the details page of the leads that
    are local (from *Canada*), which means users can only pre-qualify
    local leads. Click *Done* to go back to the visual designer.

Figure 7-64. *Setting transition criteria*

11. In the right sidebar, click on the *During* subtab to set actions
    to happen when a user clicks attempts to pre-qualify a lead
    matching the criteria above. First, check *Make Notes as
    mandatory* to ask the user to log the event (pre-qualification).
    Then click on the *Add* button and select *Company* from the
    field's drop-down list as shown in Figure 7-65.

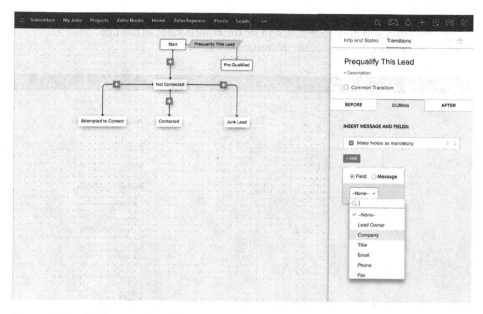

Figure 7-65. *Adding actions to happen during transition*

12. Click on the *Validation* link appearing next to the *Company* field. Then in the field validation criteria enter a single criterion: *Company, is not empty*. Also, type in an alert message as shown in Figure 7-66, so when the user skips entering the company name for a pre-qualified lead, they get an error with this message asking them to put down the company name. Click *Done* to continue.

Figure 7-66. *Adding validation criteria for the Company field*

13. In the right sidebar click Add again and similar to the previous step, add the Phone field and set the criteria for it, so it is not left empty. You can see the results in Figure 7-67.

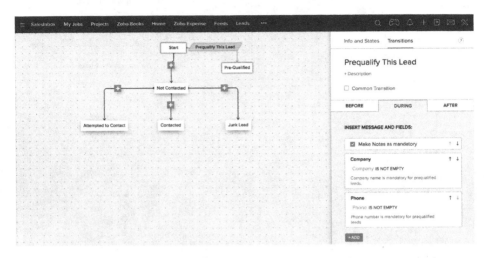

Figure 7-67. *Adding second action for the transition*

14. In the right sidebar, move to the *After* subtab (Figure 7-68) to set actions that will happen after a lead state becomes pre-qualified. In this case we want the user's supervisor to get notified via email that the user just made a lead pre-qualified. Click on *Email Alerts* link to continue.

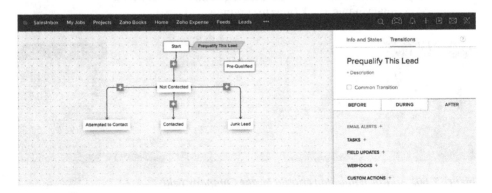

Figure 7-68. *Adding an action to happen post-transition*

15. In the Email Alert form (Figure 7-69):

    a. Enter "*Email Supervisor*" for *Name;*

    b. Under *Email Recipients,* select *People Associated with the...,* then *Lead Creator,* then *Lead Owner's Manager* from the list;

    c. Select (or create) a suitable template for the occasion and select it for *Email Template;*

    d. Select *Record Owner's Email* for *From;* and

    e. Click *Done* to proceed.

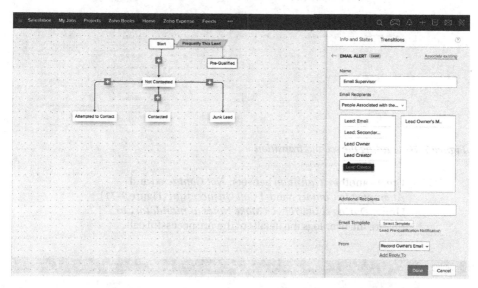

Figure 7-69. *Setting an email alert for post-transition*

16. Create a *Transition* named *Haven't Contacted Yet* between *Start* and *Not Contacted* (Figure 7-70) states and leave it without any further configuration. This means that a *Haven't Contacted Yet* button will show for all leads as a possible state, but it will not do anything specific during or after being clicked other than changing the *Lead Status* value to *Not Contacted*.

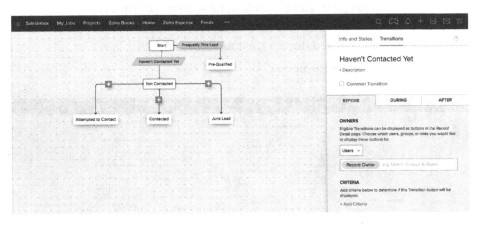

Figure 7-70. *Adding the second transition*

17. Create another *Transition* between *Not Contacted* and *Attempted to Contact* named *Call Unsuccessful* (Figure 7-71). Under *During* subtab check *Make Notes as mandatory* to ensure the user logs the details of the unsuccessful call.

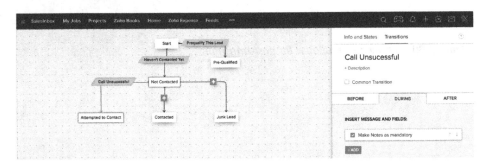

Figure 7-71. *Adding the third trnasition*

18.   Create one more *Transition* between *Not Contacted* and *Contacted* named *Call Successful* (Figure 7-72). Then check *Make Notes as mandatory* and add a criterion for *Email* field not to be left empty.

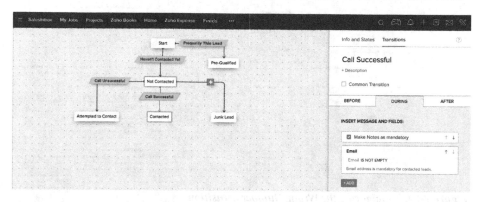

Figure 7-72. *Configuring the Call Successful transition*

19.   Also, add an *After* action to send an email alert this time to the lead themselves with a special offer template (Figure 7-73). The idea is when a user sets the *Lead Status* to contacted, they must send an email with the latest offers to the lead. This transition automates that process. Click *Done* when you are finished.

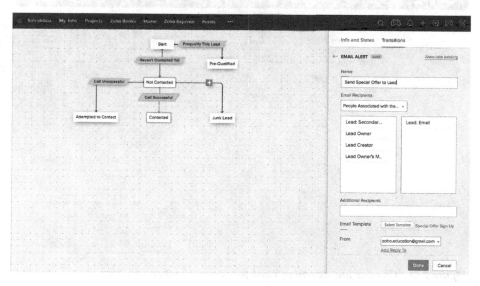

Figure 7-73. *Setting an email alert for the Call Succeful transition*

20. Finally, create a *Transition* between *Not Contacted* and *Junk Lead* named *Wrong Number* (Figure 7-74).

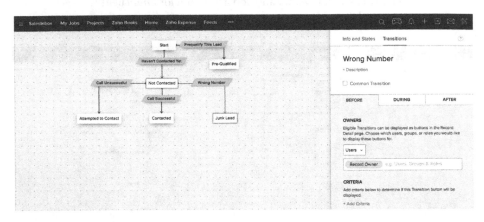

Figure 7-74. *Configuring the Wrong Number transition*

21. Under *After* subtab, create a *Task* action, so when a user sets a lead as junk, a task is created and a reminder is set for them to manually delete the leads after 30 days (Figure 7-75). Click *Done* when you are finished.

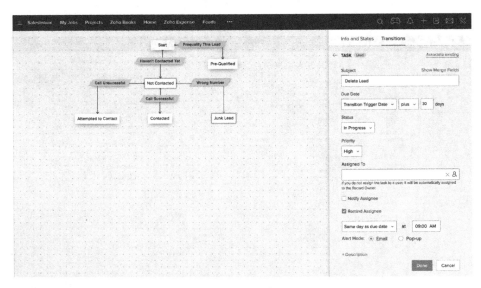

Figure 7-75. *Creating and assigning a task for Wrong Number transition*

22. Click *Save* in the bottom left of the screen to save the Blueprint process (Figure 7-76).

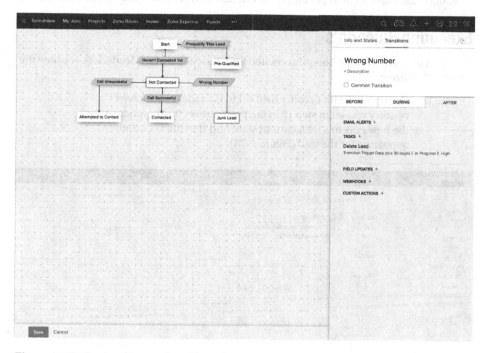

Figure 7-76. *Saving the complete Blueprint*

Et voilà! You created your first Blueprint process and it is listed in the Blueprints page. By default, it is deactivated. Click on the Status switch and activate it (Figure 7-77).

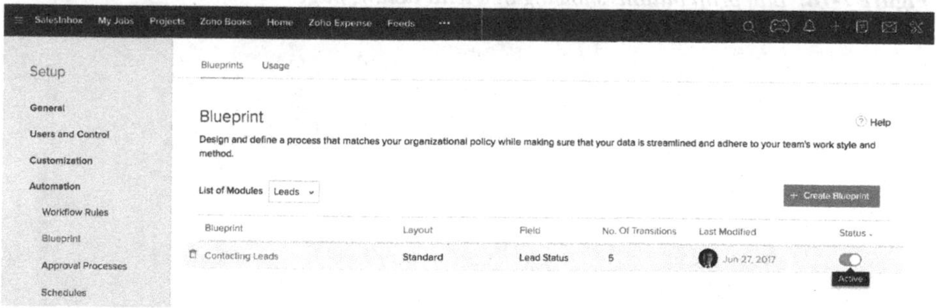

Figure 7-77. *Newly create Blueprint activated*

As you can see, creating Blueprints is quite a task, especially for more complex processes. However, it is well worth the time investment as it will save your team many hours avoiding small mistakes or forgetting procedure, and also your company's hard-earned cash.

Executing Blueprints

Now that we have a robust Blueprint created for Lead Status of the leads, let's see how the users will utilize it:

1. Open a lead with *Country* field set to Canada (or whichever country you set in step 10 in the previous section). Notice the new gray row with current state and transition buttons appearing for the lead (Figure 7-78).

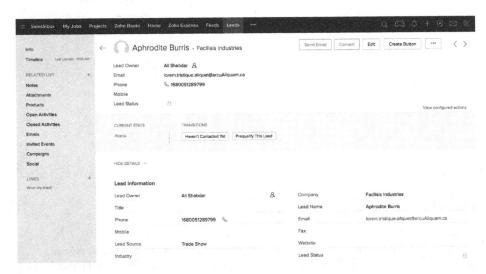

***Figure 7-78.** Blueprint buttons showing in a lead details page*

2. Click on the *View* configuration actions link on the top right of the gray row. The *Contacting Leads* dialog box will open showing the possible transitions and states for the *Lead Status* (Figure 7-79). This diagram is quite handy and acts as your pocket reference process map. Close the dialog box to continue.

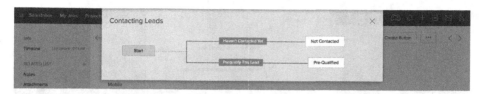

Figure 7-79. *Current process reference map*

3. Click on *Haven't Contacted Yet*. The buttons will change to a new set resembling exactly the states you designed beyond the *Not Contacted* state (Figure 7-80). The *Current State* and the *Lead Source* are both changed to *Not Contacted*. Also notice that you can't change *Lead Source* manually like you normally could. This field is now controlled by the Blueprint process.

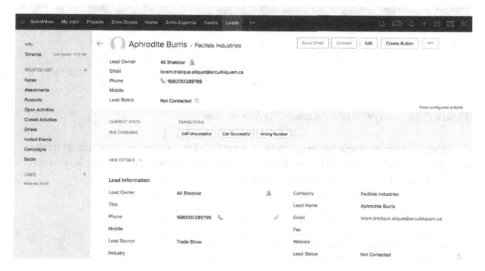

Figure 7-80. *Blueprint buttons change according to the state (Lead Source)*

4. Suppose you made a phone call and the lead picked up the
    phone. Click on the *Call Successful* button to continue down
    the process. As per our design, Blueprint will show the *Call
    Successful* dialog box asking us to log the call in the *Notes* and
    make sure *Email* field is populated (Figure 7-81). Fill in the
    blanks and click *Save* to proceed.

Figure 7-81. *Blueprint process enforces data entry upon a successful call*

At this stage our feisty Blueprint process has completed its task enforcing a number
of rules and guiding user behavior.

Before we move on, there is another place in CRM that you can check all approvals
and processes that await your action in one place. It is called My Jobs and is accessible
from the top menu bar (Figure 7-82).

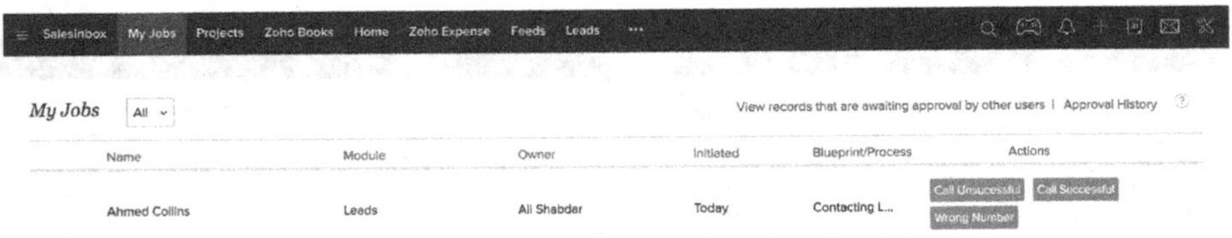

Figure 7-82. *Blueprint process under My Jobs section*

Here, you can review the items in the list and click on an appropriate action button
to move the work forward in the underlying process workflow. In this example, you can
see a (Blueprint) process initiated and waiting for your command.

Blueprint Usage Reports

Blueprint provides you with a number of reports and stats as to how existing processes are being used. You can access usage reports in the Blueprint page under Usage tab (Figure 7-83).

Figure 7-83. *Blueprints usage reports*

One of these reports, for instance, is the Transition Occurrences, which shows a bar chart for the number of transitions happening for each state of a specific Blueprint (Figure 7-84).

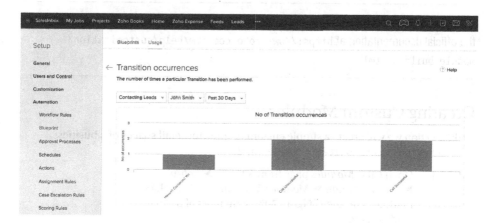

Figure 7-84. *Transaction Occurrences report for the Blueprint*

Knowing these stats will help you design a better process map knowing where the heavy loads are and at which stage (if any) processes are dropped or underperform for any reason.

To take this further, these reports could also help you improve your real-life processes by finding and addressing bottlenecks and other issues. After all, Blueprint processes and other workflows in the CRM must simulate real-life business processes.

■ **Reference**   You can learn more about Blueprint, its features, and limitations in the official documentation: `https://www.zoho.com/crm/help/blueprint/`.

Custom Modules

Zoho CRM offers a decent collection of modules that in most cases addresses all your business needs. *Leads*, *Contacts*, *Accounts*, and *Deal*, are just some of the standard CRM modules. However, every business has unique requirements and CRM allows you to accommodate these unique requirements.

It is possible to customize the standard modules by adding and removing fields specific to your business, and changing value, validation rules, or behavior of these modules. For instance, you can make *First Name* mandatory for *Leads*, change list and order of *Stages* in *Deals*, and add a new *Mother Company* field to *Accounts*.

However, if the existing modules don't serve your purpose, it is also possible to create new modules from the ground up. Suppose you run a real estate operation and need to maintain a full list of all your properties with fields such as size, floor, bedrooms, etc. Or you need to have access to actionable market data from within CRM.

Not only will custom modules allow you to create and maintain various lists of information in the CRM, they interact well with the data stored in other CRM modules. For example, you can add a field to your real estate module called *Agent* and have it populate from CRM users, or attach a real estate record to a deal.

■ **Reference**   You can learn more about the ins and out of customizing CRM modules in the official documentation at `https://www.zoho.com/crm/help/customization/module-builder.html`.

Creating Custom Modules

In this section we will create a simple custom module for retail spaces of a business.
Follow these steps to create a custom module:

1. Open CRM *Modules* page from *Settings* ➤ *Setup* ➤ *Customization* ➤ *Modules*. You can see all available modules are listed (Figure 7-85) with most of them configurable.

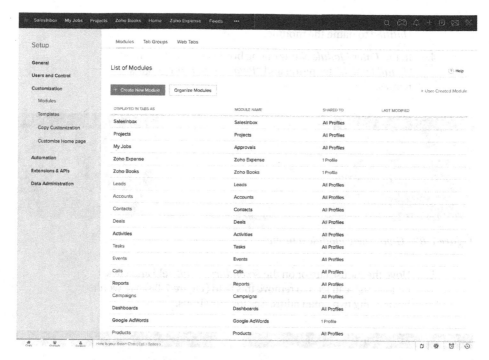

Figure 7-85. *List of existing modules*

2. Click on the Create New Module button on top of the list. Create New Module page will open (Figure 7-86). On the left, there is a sidebar with different types of fields that you can use in the module. The rest of the page is allocated to the module designer where you can decide what fields the module will have and design how the module will look like in the details view.

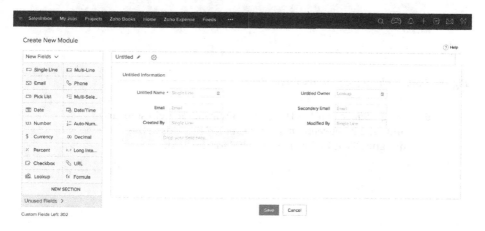

Figure 7-86. *Module designer*

3. Click on the top of the module designer where it reads *Untitled* to name the module.

4. In the *Enter Module Name* dialog box (Figure 7-87), enter "*Retail Outlets*" for plural and "*Retail Outlet*" for singular names.

Figure 7-87. *Giving new module a name*

5. Hove the mouse cursor on the *Secondary Email* field and click on the trash can icon to remove this field (Figure 7-88). We won't be needing two email addresses for our shops.

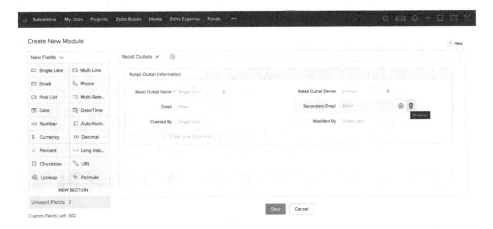

Figure 7-88. *Deleting Secondary Email field*

6. Drag a *Single Line* field (Figure 7-89) from the right sidebar and drop it between *Email* and *Created By* fields in the designer. Type in *Street* as the label for the field.

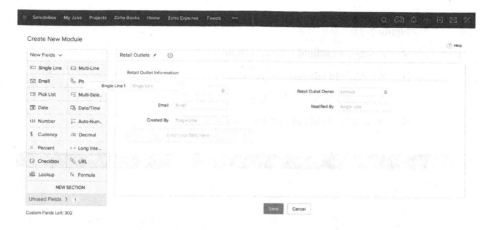

Figure 7-89. *Dragging a field and dropping it onto the designer*

7. Drag and drop a *Pick List* field to the form right below the *Street* field. In the Picklist properties dialog box, type in "*City*" in *Field Label*, add a number of cities under *Pick List Options*, and make the field *Required* as shown in Figure 7-90. Click Done to continue.

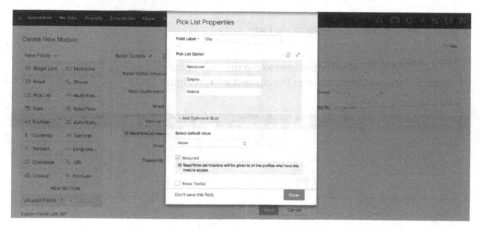

Figure 7-90. *Setting Pick List propoerties*

8.   Add more fields to the designer and order them as shown in
      Figure 7-91:

   a.   A *Single Line* field labeled *Phone,*

   b.   A *URL* field labeled *Google Map,*

   c.   A *Number* field labeled *Capacity*, and

   d.   A *Number* field labeled *Number of Staff.*

Figure 7-91. *Adding more fields to the form*

9.   Click the gear button next to the module name and select
      Module Permissions in the context menu (Figure 7-92).

Figure 7-92. *Setting module permissions*

10. In the Module Permission dialog box (Figure 7-93), click the text box and then add *Staff* from the context menu, so both *Staff* members can access this module. Click *Save* to continue.

Figure 7-93. *Allowing Staff members to access the module*

Once you are done designing the module, click *Save* on the bottom of the page to create the module.

Accessing Custom Modules

Custom modules are accessible from the top menu bar. Find *Retail Outlets* item in the menu bar (it may be hidden under the ...) and click on it. An empty module page will open inviting you to add or import retail outlets (Figure 7-94).

Figure 7-94. *Newly created module page*

Clicking on the *Create Retail Outlet* will bring the corresponding form (Figure 7-95) waiting for you to create a new entry.

Figure 7-95. *Creating a new Retail Outlet*

The interface and the look and feel are almost identical to other CRM modules, making it easy to use. Almost all standard features, such as views, filters, import and export, and printing, etc., are available to custom modules. You can attach files and associate activities to the custom module records.

Custom modules will help you put key information lists in one place next to other important information. No more decentralized and conflicting lists of company information floating around in random Excel files.

Extending CRM Beyond Zoho Platform

As you learned in the previous chapter, you can extend the power of Zoho CRM by integrating it with other Zoho Apps, such as Creator, Books, and Project. You can also connect CRM to external apps, such as Google AdWords and Slack.

But there are times when you still need more external apps and services to work with Zoho CRM seamlessly. For instance, if you already use a third-party accounting app, or custom enterprise software, you would want to automatically exchange data between CRM and them.

Fortunately Zoho offers a REST (Representational State Transfer) API (Application Programming Interface) that allows you to send and receive data between CRM and third-party apps that support APIs.

You (or your software developer) can use this API with common programming and scripting languages, such as Python, Java, PHP, and C# and create apps that interact with CRM, or create middleware that connects CRM with other software.

This is not a job for the faint of heart and you need to be an experienced programmer or have access to one (or more). As a business owner or decision maker, rest assured that it is possible to create interoperability between Zoho CRM and other advanced software.

■ **Reference** Since this is an advanced topic and chances are that you are already bored, I am not going to go any deeper than an honorable mention of the CRM API and will refer you to the official documentation at `https://www.zoho.com/crm/help/api/welcome.html`.

Summary

In this chapter, you learned how to control access to CRM data down to record levels using users, roles, groups, and data sharing rules.

You also learned a great deal about automating business processes using workflows, approvals, and the all-new Blueprint.

Another key learning point was the custom modules that will help you bring all organizational information stored in scattered lists under one roof and manage them properly.

We also quickly touched on extending Zoho CRM beyond the Zoho suite using REST API and custom programming.

■ **Reference** Zoho CRM regularly introduces new features. In fact, a number of features were released while I was writing this book, and I'm happy I could touch on some of the major ones, such as *Sales Inbox* and *Blueprint*. Make sure you visit the What's New page on the Zoho CRM website at `https://www.zoho.com/crm/whats-new/` to see what exciting features are added to the CRM.

One More Thing

I hope this book helps you win big with Zoho CRM. Whether you are setting up CRM for your organization from the ground up, or providing consultation to a client, always keep in mind that you cannot and should not rely solely on information solutions, including CRM, to improve your business.

The most important factor for the success of any information solution is the people who will be using it. If you train your people patiently, and manage the transition from the previous system to the new one properly, the probability of success for the new system will dramatically increase.

However, if you just go out and pay an arm and a leg to buy the best CRM (or any other information system) in the market only to throw it at your team to use it without getting the buy-in of the managers and onboarding other staff, don't blame your inevitable failure on the poor software.

I have seen companies that were struggling with their existing software and all they did to remedy that was to buy (or create) more software.

If you want to succeed, give People, Process, and Technology the same weight in your decision making. Let your team see that you (as a decision maker) are doing this for them – not to them. Make sure you involve the right people in the organization from the early stages, when you are mapping processes and choosing solutions.

Never underestimate the power of human resistance as the most sophisticated software is as useless as an empty gun if people refuse to use it properly. It is no surprise that the subject of Change Management is such a hot topic in the corporate environment.

And finally, if you are in charge of a big operation, don't shy away from involving external, experienced consultants who know business process management; change management; organizational behavior; and, of course, CRM.

Good luck.

Index

A

Automating business processes
- approvals automation, 205–206, 208–209, 211–213
- features, 196
- workflow automation
    - activities/processes, 197
    - rules, creation, 198–204

B

Blueprint
- creation, 213–222, 224–225
- execution, 226–228
- usage reports, 229

Business forecasting, 126–130

Business process apps
- AppCreator, 12
- Creator, 11
- reports, 13
- Site24x7, 13

Business process management (BPM), 24

Business process model and notation (BPMN), 26

C, D

Campaign management
- add leads and contacts, 137–138
- creation, 132–135
- customizing, 135–136

Converting qualified leads
- account creation, 95
- contact creation, 95
- deals
    - creation, 97
    - customizing stages, 100–101
    - homepage dashboard, 99–100
    - stage up to date, 98
    - viewing, 98–99
- details page, 93
- output, 94

Customer relationship management (CRM)
- BPM, 24
- BPMN, 26
- business operation, 22–23
- Camunda Modeler, 27
- definition, 21
- ERP, 23
- mapping business processes, 25–26
- optimization, 22
- process, 24

Custom modules
- accessing, 235
- creation, 230–234

E

Email and collaboration apps
- BugTracker, 9
- chat, 11
- connect, 9
- Docs, 8
- mail, 7
- meeting, 10
- notebook, 8
- project, 9
- Showtime, 11
- vault, 10

Enterprise resource planning (ERP), 23

© Ali Shabdar 2017
A. Shabdar, *Mastering Zoho CRM*, DOI 10.1007/978-1-4842-2904-0

■ F

Finance apps
  books, 13
  expense, 15
  inventory, 15
  invoice, 14
  subscriptions, 14

■ G

Google AdWords, 155

■ H

Help desk apps
  assist, 16
  desk, 15
  mobile device management, 17
  ServiceDesk Plus, 16
Homepage, 42
Human resources apps
  people, 18
  recruit, 17

■ I, J, K

ITapps. *See* Help desk apps

■ L

Lead management
  bulk operations
    mass transferring leads, 81–82
    mass updating leads, 77–81
  importing multiple leads, 71–73, 75–77
  interaction, 68, 70–71
  lead creation, 65
  lead page, 67
Leads finding
  filtering, 85
  searching, 83–84
  views
    customizing, 87–89
    custom views, creating, 90, 92
Leads module, 65

■ M, N, O

Marketing
  campaignmanagement (*see* Campaign
    management)

customer feedback, 156
  definition, 131
  email marketing, 155
  social media, 156
  Webforms (*see* Webforms)
Mass email
  feature, 151–154
  schedule, 154

■ P

Process mapping
  BPMN 2.0, 28–29
  cold calling procedure
    activity, 32, 36
    Camunda Modeler, 31
    connecting, 33
    end event, 37
    gateway, 34–35
    overlapping, 37–38
    start event, 33
Purchase order (PO), 116

■ Q

Quotes
  conversion
    quotes to sales orders, 116–117
    sales orders to invoices, 117–120
  creation, deal
    adding products, 104
    product form, 104
    quote and address information, 103
    quote listed, 107
    saving, 106
    second product creation, 105
  customized templates
    HTML and CSS, 110–115
  emailing, 107–109

■ R

Reports
  creation
    different file formats, 126
    filter selecting, 125
    information columns, 124
    picking report type, 123
    report in action, 126
    report name and description, 125
    source modules selecting, 123
    tabular format selecting, 124

default reports list, 121
favorite, 121
lead by status report, 122
pipeline, stage report, 122

■ S

Sales and marketing apps
    campaigns, 4
    contact manager, 6
    CRM, 2–3
    forms, 6
    motivator, 7
    SalesInbox, 3
    SalesIQ, 3
    sites, 5
    social media, 5
    survey, 4
Sales force automation, 63–64
Sales order (SO), 116
Sales pipeline managing
    lead qualification, 62
    leads, 62
    opportunities, 63
Security management
    data sharing
        campaigns information, 187
        default permissions, 189–190
        record-level sharing, 193
        rules, 190–191, 193
        types, access levels, 188
    groups, 194–196
    profiles, 180–183
    roles, 184–187
    users, 178–179
Setting up, Zoho CRM
    configuration, 46–51
    email settings, 54–55, 57
    personal Settings, 47

SalesInbox enabling, 58–60
setup page, 47
tools context menu, 46
user management, 51–53

■ T, U, V

Template editor, 111
Typical sales pipeline, 61–62

■ W, X, Y

Webforms creation
    company, 141
    email, 140–141
    embed options, 150
    form configuration, 149
    lead, 142
    merge fields, 147
    notification, 144
    template gallery, 145–146

■ Z

Zoho CRM
    account creation, 40
    company information updation, 42
    Creator, 173–175
    enabling authentication, 41
    Finance Suite, 167, 169–172
    homepage, 40, 42
    mail, 160–163
    modules, 44–45
    projects, 163–165, 167
    terminology
        account, 44
        contact, 44
        deal, 44
        lead, 44

Get the eBook for only $5!

Why limit yourself?

With most of our titles available in both PDF and ePUB format, you can access your content wherever and however you wish—on your PC, phone, tablet, or reader.

Since you've purchased this print book, we are happy to offer you the eBook for just $5.

To learn more, go to http://www.apress.com/companion or contact support@apress.com.

Apress®

Printed in the United States
By Bookmasters